# A STUDY OF SAMĀSASVARA AND SAMĀSĀNTA SUFFIXATION IN THE AṢṬĀDHYĀYĪ OF PĀṆINĪ

# A STUDY OF SAMĀSASVARA AND SAMĀSĀNTA SUFFIXATION IN THE AṢṬĀDHYĀYĪ OF PĀṆINĪ

*By*

G. GAYATHRI PREETHA

BHARATIYA KALA PRAKASHAN
DELHI (INDIA)

First Edition : 2008



*Published by* **C.P. Gautam**
**BHARATIYA KALA PRAKASHAN**
3421-A, IInd Floor, Narang Colony,
Tri Nagar, Delhi-110035.
Phone : 32967505, Telefax : 011-27393083
E-mail : bkp3421@yahoo.co.in

**ISBN : 978-81-8090-204-8**

*Laser Type Setting by*
A-ONE GRAPHICS
Pitampura, Delhi-110088

*Printed By :*
BDH Printer at Salasar Imaging Systems
Delhi.

*for my parents*

# FOREWORD

Grammarians of Classical Languages have traditionally engaged in the study of accent. They have long since been concerned about the semantic and phonological aspects of the accent. It is especially true of the Indian tradition that the Veda has been examined threadbare with respect to accent or supra-segmentals. With the dawn of Modern Linguistics, the study has taken a significant turn in phonological and semantic studies. The relation between semantic and phonological bases is a present day focus of linguists, Indian and abroad. Dr. G. Gayathri Preetha took up for her doctoral disseration the semantic basis of compositional suffixation in compounds ie. Samāsānta suffixation in samāsa, in Sanskrit. Her emphasis has been on providing evidence directly from the Aṣṭādhyāyī of Pāṇini with the help of the Bhāṣya commentatorial tradition. In the main, this book collates evidence for the accentuation brought about by the process of samāsānta suffixation in the Aṣṭādhyāyī of Pāṇini.

Starting with an introduction to the general nature of accent or Svara in the Veda, she in Chapter two covers the nature of Samāsānta in the commentatorial tradition. The various examples of Pāṇinian samāsāntas are also provided in this chapter with meticulous attention to detail. The entire commentatorial tradition on how the tatpuruṣa or determinative compound and the bahuvrīhi or exocentric compound differ, is dealt with in Chapter three with considerable skill.

The relation of accent and samāsānta to other grammatical affixes such as verbal affixes, past passive participles and case affixes are also dealt with in the following pages. Her treatment of the relationship between accent, samāsānta and case affix or vibhakti is noteworthy, borrowing heavily from the Mahābhāṣya. In the final chapter, she has summed up her conclusions and shows evidence for the semantic basic of accentuation, which is the thrust of this book.

While there has been an unbroken investigation into accent in Indian linguistics, a need of further exploration of accent vis-ā-vis compositional suffixation has been met with by this book. Dr. G. Gayathri Preetha has presented a neat and scholarly work, well executed in format. Her dissertation was commended to the University of Madras by Prof. George Cardona, Professor Emeritus, University of Pennsylvania, U.S.A. I have great pleasure in recommending it to all serious students of grammar.

Chennai-5
26th May 2007

**(Sinirudha Dash)**
Professor and Head,
Dept. of Sanskrit,
University of Madras.

# ACKNOWLEDGMENTS

I am deeply indebted to Dr. Siniruddha Dash, Professor and Head, Department of Sanskrit, Oriental Research Institute, University of Madras, Chennai - 5, for his guidance through the academic process. Professor Dash's critical but gentle suggestions have egged me on the path of excellence and independence. By being an exemplar teacher he has motivated me into discovering the joy of creativity in grammatical endeavour. I also thank Professor Dash for providing me with a UGC Project Fellowship which has contributed to my appreciation of advanced academic study. I am grateful to be one of his students.

I thank the University of Madras for providing me the Lady K. Srinivasa Aiyangar Endowment Scholarship for a period of two years.

I thank the teaching faculty of the Sanskrit Department, University of Madras for their encouragement and expository lectures on varied aspects of the Sanskrit Language.

I thank Professor M. H. Sastri, Retired Principal, Sanskrit College, Thiruvananthapuram, for his insightful elucidation of the subtleties of sections of the Mahābhāṣyam.

I thank Dr. P. Visalakshi, Director, Oriental Research Institute, University of Kerala, Kariavattom, Thiruvananthapuram, for providing me the introduction to Professor M. H. Sastri

I am extremely grateful to Professor K.V. Sharma, Director, Sri Sarada Education Society, Adyar, Chennai-20, who generously provided bibliographical references.

I wish to record my sincere gratitude to Dr. Mamata Mishra for checking the manuscript and her patient reading of several drafts of the thesis.

I thank all the members of Adyar Library, Theosophical Institute, Chennai, Kuppuswamy Sastri Research Institute Library, Chennai, ORI Library (University of Madras) Chennai, University of Madras (Main) Library, Chennai, Deccan College Library, Pune, Centre for Advanced Studies in Sanskrit, Pune, Bhandarkar Oriental Research Institute, Pune, for their gracious help in locating journals and books pertinent to the research of this thesis.

I thank Mr. Babu Rajendran and Mrs. Sornalatha for their assistance in the administrative process.

I thank Om Enterprises and Student Xerox for their patient help.

I am grateful to my father P.S. Ganesan who made appropriate changes in diction and style, often acting as an amaneunsis.

I am aware of the support from my siblings Usha, Jayashree, Ravi; my simple thanks to them. I wish to acknowledge the support given by Mangalam, Pushpa and Professor R. Rangarajan. A word of thanks to Dr. N. Rangarajan. To all my friends who believed that I would complete this first step, I convey my heartfelt gratitude.

I am deeply grateful to Mr. C.P. Gautam of Bharatiya Kala Prakashan for bearing up with the delay in publishing this book. Without his patience and encouragement this publication would not have seen the light of the day.

# PREFACE

During my study of the Samarthāhnika as a graduate student, the topic of samāsānta suffixation and samāsasvara seemed intriguing and full of possibility for further study. An intial survey indicated a lacuna in this area with regard to study in this topic using the commentatorial tradition. A survey of research on Pāṇini by G. Cardona confirmed a paucity of study done in this area vis-à-vis internal evidence and commentatorial evidence. The survey also pointed to seminal work carried out by M.D. Balasubrahmaniam on the nature of krt accentuation. This encouraged the adoption of a similar approach to accentuation of compounds with reference to the Aṣṭādhyāyī. Consequently, much of M.D. Balasubrahmaniam's work has been cited as reference to appropriate sections of this thesis.

While taking up this topic for further study I was well aware that considerable work has been done on the Indo-European aspects of samāsānta. Here, we hope to present a synthesis of compositional suffixation and accentuation using the commentaries on samāsānta suffixation and the formation of samāsasvara. Both Devanāgari and Roman diacritics have been used through the text of the thesis.

It is my humble hope that this thesis submitted to the University of Madras as a docotoral disertation, is a significant contribution in the area.

**G. Gayathri Preetha**

# ABBREVIATIONS

| | | |
|---|---|---|
| A | : | Aṣṭhādhyāyī |
| Kāś | : | Kāśikā |
| Mbh | : | Mahābhāṣyam |
| Pdm | : | Padamañjarī |
| P | : | Pāṇini |
| RV | : | Ṛg Veda |
| SK | : | Siddhāntakaumudī |
| SSC | : | Svarasiddhāntacandrikā |
| TS | : | Taittirīya Saṁhitā |
| T.I | : | Table 1 p. 141 |

# CONTENTS

# AIM AND SCOPE OF THE BOOK

A critical review of the available literature concerning the aspects of *samāsānta* suffixation and *samāsasvara* reveals a certain lacuna in the area. This encouraged me to take up this topic for further study. Moreover, no previous work has been carried out connecting the two essential aspects in the light of the commentatorial tradition. It is my humble hope that it will be a significant though preliminary contribution in this area.

The aim of this thesis is two fold:

1. To provide internal evidence in the *Aṣṭādhyāyī* (A), with evidence from the *Māhābhāṣya (Mbh),* for *samāsānta* suffixation. Patañjali's description and evaluation of the importance of accentuation in *tatpuruṣ a (tp)* and *bahuvrīhi (bv)* serve as the back drop, from which a case for *samāsānta* suffixation and accentuation in *samāsa (samāsasvara)* is made. The interdependence of compositional suffixation and accentuation is the essence of this work.

2. The nature and motivation of semantic influences on the phonology of compound words is briefly and secondarily highlighted. The manner, mode and degree to which semantics governs *samāsasvara* is described in relation to morphology as well.

All evidence is culled from the traditional sources and the inferences are based on the internal relations of *sūtra-s* and the contents of the *A*.

Otto Bohtlingk describes *samāsānta* in *A* 5.4.68 as "ohne die bedeutung desselben zu andern". George Cardona hints at the senseless nature of the *samāsānta* in his study of bases, affixes and meaning. Dipti Sharma treats *samāsānta* as an *atyantasvārthika pratyaya* (cf. Chapter 2). From a purely formal criterion the suffix is semantically irrelevant. However, in the light of Patañjali's synthesis in the *Samarthāhnika* an attempt is made here to provide an explanation for the relationship of *samāsānta* and the *udātta* that contribute to the unitary accent of the *samāsa*.

The relationship of the *udātta* accent to the *samāsānta* suffix which is added and then elided in the final stage of compound word formation is a complex one. To analyze the influence of the semantic condition on the nature of *svara* on the *pūrvapada* or *uttarapada* of the *bv* or *tp* compound adds a third dimension to the problem that begs many questions. Critical to the understanding of the problem are the following foremost questions.

1. The *udātta* being irrevocably linked to the *samāsānta* as the *samāsāntodātta* is discussed in the *Mbh* and is described to be influenced by meaning preconditions observed by *Pāṇini (P),* which govern the placement of accent on the compound. The analysis is to identify the patterns of these relationships as discussed in the *Mbh* with respect to semantics and morphology.

2. A more complex problem is that of the *samāsānta* suffix itself. In the strict formal Paninian tradition these are defined as *taddhita* suffixes devoid of any meaning, carrying a voided sense or null meaning.

   However both the *Samarthāhnika* and the *Mbh* (on *A* 5.4.68, 6.1.223, 6.2.1, 6.2.2...) discuss the semantic conditions laid down for the suffixation process and the accentuation. Such being the case wih respect to its important contribution to the formation of *samāsāntodātta* the discussion of the *samāsānta* suffix will have to be tackled from two levels - one at a purely formal and morphological level as the *prakriyā* defines it and from the semantic which is viewed in the *Mbh*.

3. The more general area of the problem of *svara* is that of accentuation itself and the limitation to which Pāṇinian grammar is exposed in this area. Accentuation has been a controversial topic but the consensual agreement has been that even P's attempt to document fully the accent of the *Veda* falls short of the goal he must have set out for himself. Not withstanding this fact, this work confines itself to an exploration of *svara* as detailed in *P*'s *A*.

# REVIEW OF LITERATURE

## 0.1 The Traditional Commentatorial Approach

दुष्टः शब्दः स्वरतो वर्णतो वा
मिथ्या प्रयुक्तो न तमर्थम् आह ।
स वाग्वज्रो यजमानं हिनस्ति
यथेन्द्रशत्रु स्वरतोऽपराधात् ॥

Patañjali in the instruction of the purpose of *vyākaraṇa* makes his observation of the importance of accentuation. Indeed, he goes on to expatiate on the importance of *svara* and the importance of accentuation and the knowledge of grammar that serves as an aid to the accentuation of the vedic.

### 0.1.1 Pāṇini

*P* included accentual rules in the total of 3997 (including the *Śiva-sūtra-s)* in the *A*. *"P* devotes 3980 rules according to my count to a systematic study of the accentuation of the secular *(bhāṣā)* and the sacred *(chandas)* speech."[1]

P assigns the Chapter 6.2 to the rules of accentuation of compounds *(samāsasvara)*. In order to comprehend *samāsasvara* one needs, requires a knowledge of the *dhātusvara, pratyayasvara* and the nature of the *IT* accent. *P* defines the *udātta* (high tone), the *anudātta* (the low tone), and *svarita* (the circumflex) according to the designatory definitions provided by the antecedent *Prātiśākhya-s*. Although *P* does not explicitly describe the phonemic contrasts brought about by suprasegmentals, he does use the device in presupposing the function of accent.[2]

Following *P,* were Kātyāyana and Patañjali. Kātyāyana supplements P's *svara sūtra-s* where he feels the instance deserves to be buttressed by evidence from usage. The *Mbh* is of particular importance to this work as it is Patañjali who synthesizes discrete elements in the *A* to present a case of *svara, samāsānta, saṁkhyā, liṅga* in the *Samarthāhnika*. Here, an attempt is made to substantiate the relations shown by Patañjali by using the internal evidence of the *A* and the glosses of the commentaries.

### 0.1.2 *prakriyā* Commentaries

Bhaṭṭoji Dīkṣita rearranged the accentual rules of *P* into 266 vedic rules and 329 accentual rules. The former is known as the *vaidika - prakriyā* and the latter the *svara -prakriyā*. Bhaṭṭoji closely follows the *Mbh* and divides his text as

साधारणस्वर, धातुस्वर, प्रातिपदिकस्वर, फिट्स्वर, प्रत्ययस्वर, समासस्वर, तिङन्तस्वर

Nāgēśa too comments on the accentual rules in the *Laghuśabdēnduśēkhara*.

#### 0.1.2.1 *svara* Manuals

Though major independent treatises on accentuation are not available, some of the accentual treatises that have come down to us are *Svaraśirōmaṇi, Svarāṅkuśa, Svaraprakriyā, Svaraprakāśa, Svarakaumudī, Svaramañjarī, Svarasiddhānta-candrikā* (M.D. Balasubrahmaniam,1981).

The *Svaramañjarī* is often confused with the explicatory compilation of verses by T.B. Abhyankar.[3] The independent treatise however is the *Svarasiddhāntamañjarī* of *Nṛsimha* (edited by G.V. Devasthali).[4] This treatise deals with the *samāsasvara* in the तृतीयः परिच्छेदः (the third chapter).

*Svarasiddhāntacandrikā (SSC)* is an extremely useful manual compiled by Śrinivāsa Yajvan where he discusses the Pāṇinian rules thoroughly with respect to *svara* providing attestation from the *Taittirīya Saṁhitā*.[5] Often he criticizes the position taken by *Nṛsimha* (author of the *Svarasiddhānta-mañjarī)* on the views of accentuation of the illustrations from the *Taittirīya Saṁhitā (TS)*.

*Svaraprakriyā* of Ramacandra Śeṣa is a popular treatise calculated to be written hundred years after Bhaṭṭoji.[6]

"It can be ascertained that if the accent of a compound is available and is in conformity to linguistic and P's rules the compound then authentically belongs to the vedic. If the accent is lost then surely it belongs to a period other than the vedic. If the accent shows ambiguity in form or meaning then it reflects a period of the vedic in the decline" (M.D.Pandit, 1989).

**0.2 Twentieth Century Indian Scholarship:**

The attempts to deal with accentuation in vedic has been a long standing one; there exists a thread of synthesis from the works of Indo-European (IE) scholars whose efforts included an approach based on the study of the *Pāṇinīya* commentatorial tradition and the early twentieth century attempts of scholars to use the exegetical works of Sāyaṇa, Bhaṭṭabhāskara or Mādhva to explain their views on accent.

This review of literature on the problem of accentuation starts with an introduction to the questions raised by such scholars as Sankaran, Ananthanarayana, Laddu and Varma. The antecedent work of Western scholarship is being taken up later in the sequence with the intention of emphasizing traditional treatment as *a priori'* to the crux of this thesis. Bhattacarya provides an explanation of the term *"Chandas"* and the etymology of the word.[7]

The problem of accentuation is unique to the *Veda* for it is found only in the *Saṁhitā* and *Brāhmaṇa-s* losing its force of application although it is found even in the time of the *Āraṇyaka-s*. The accent thus dwindled away and by the development of the Classical Sanskrit literature ceased to exist as a viable functional phonological element. The study of accent *(svara)* has been often confounded by the lack of independent treatises written with specific detail to its function in the *Veda*. The earliest sources of laws of accentuation date back to *Yāska, P*, the latter whose time is largely believed to be contemporaneous with the *Aitareya Brāhmaṇa*. According to some scholars given this background it is difficult to accept the validity of *P's* accentual rules *in toto*. The problem becomes particularly acute as several scholars of repute point to a lack of clarity and precision in the accentual rules of the *A*. In its treatment of accentuation, the penetrating precision that is the hallmark of the *A,* seems to be lacking. It is however worthwhile to consider Varma's[8] and Thieme's observations on P's accentual rules according to whom Pāṇini can account for vedic usage.

A survey of compound words is treated by Murti.[9] Compositional suffixation is treated by Roland.[10] There exists a body of work of considerable volume supporting Pāṇinian accentual description as well as the semantic basis for accent. Kunhan Raja[11] shows the relation between semantics and accent. C.R. Sankaran relates accentual variation to semantic variation. He stresses the function of accent as a morphological element in their "speech consciousness".[12] Dealing specifically with the *"tama"* and *"tara"* morphemes (superlatives) he demonstrates the presence and function of *svara.* It is of interest that he quotes extensively the exegetes, Sāyaṇa, Mādhavabhaṭ ṭa and Skanda Svāmin with reference to the occurence of *purutamam* where *"tama"* is used in the sense of "fade away".

Two words with the same morphological form are distinguished by the accentuation of the lexeme. For आशा॑ signifies "quarters" whereas आ॒शा signifies "hope". It is accentual marking that makes clear variations of readings such as इदं मधु॑ for इदं मधुरम् of the *Kāṭhaka Saṁhitā*. S.R. Sehgal has listed such further variations between the *Saṁhitā-s* such as

ब्रह्मद्वेष (ऋसं 8, 45, 23) but ब्रह्माद्विषम् (सांस 2, 82), ऋत वाच (कपिष्ठलसं 4, 6) but ते वाचो (काठकसं 6, 7), भामितः (ऋसं 1, 114, 8) but भामिनः (वाजसं 16, 16,)[13]

He argues that it is accent *(svara)* that maintains the integrity of the morphological form, the meaning and the relation between the two. To provide evidence for his theory he has taken up the example of देवकृतम्. This illustration is of special significance to this thesis as it is pertinent to some of the arguments proposed regarding the accentuation of *tp* and *bv*. देवकृतम् in its attestation in the *Veda* can be a *bv* or *tp*; as *bv* the intended desired meaning of the poet *(A* 6.2.1) is conveyed but the exegetes have explained it as सप्तमीतत्पुरुष समास (A 6.2.2). In the TS the same passage occurs as *tp* in *TS* 3.2.5.7. It is also explained as *bv*. For the purpose of illustrating the function of accent the passage is annotated from Bhaṭṭ abhāskara -

देवादिविषये यदस्माभिः कृतमेनः अधमेः तस्यावयजनं नाशनम् असि। क्षेपे इति सप्तम्या समास सप्तमीपूर्वपदप्रकृतिस्वरत्वम् (Pā 2.9.46)

यद्वा देवादिभिः अस्मद्विषये यत्कृतमेनः फलं दुखं तस्यावयवजनमसि। तृतीया कर्मणि (Pā 6.2.47) इति पूर्वपदप्रकृतिस्वरत्वम्। ( भट्टभास्कर )

M.D. Balasubrahmaniam also quotes the exegetes in their interpretation of the word *ārya*[14]

| | | |
|---|---|---|
| ā́rya | (1) | Sāyaṇa RV 1.33.3 & AV 6.63.R Uvaṭa & Mahīdhara to VS 26.3 |
| āryá | (2) | Uvaṭa & Mahīdhara to VS 26.2<br>Sāyaṇa & Bhaṭṭabhāskara to TA 1.27.6 |
| ârya | (3) | Sāyaṇa RV 1.123.1 & TB 2.6.6.2 Bhaṭṭ abhāskara, TS 1.8.3.1 |

He argues that the exegetes have maintained consistency in adhering to the Pāṇinian position.

As a logical progression of the consideration of these works, mention has to be made of the views of S.D. Laddu on the *laukika, vaidika* and *yājñika* accentuation of the *munitraya* of Sanskrit grammar.[15] He argues that the *bhāṣā-svara* (Bh-Sv in his terminology) is the accent peculiar to the *Brāhmaṇa* and is of the nature of only acute and grave *(dvaisvara),* a modification of the *trai* of the *Saṁhitā-s*. We repeat here the conclusions, reached by him at the end of his observations.

1. Sacrificial utterance was in parts specialised vedic Sanskrit and in parts specialised spoken Sanskrit.

2. Utmost attention to accuracy in pronounciation (including accentuation) was required during sacrifice.
3. At some (probably early) stage, *mantra-'s* might have been uttered with *trai* in a sacrifice.
4. The so called *EK* during a sacrifice was probably a uniformly loud voice employed in recitation of the vedic *mantras;* the loudness helped little to make out the distinction of *trai*
5. By the time of *P,* this *EK* mode of recitation was optionally extended to the utterance of vedic *mantras* even outside the sacrificial context i.e. during the daily lesson.
6. Probably later than *P,* the Bh-Sv[16] accentuation was introduced while reciting the *Brāhmaṇa* texts including the *mantras* occuring therein.
7. *Kay* the grammarian mentions *(Vpr)* though not in his *Vārttikas*. *Pt* is silent about it.
8. *Jaimini* discards the use of *Bh* for *mantras* in the *Saṁhitā* section but permits to it.

At this juncture, it would be appropriate to deal with some of the problems of accentuation. Siddheswar Varma demonstrated that *P* 's accentual rules are helpful and are adequate descriptions of the vedic accent. In yet another instance he provides a description of the vedic accent. H.S. Anantharnarayana brings out the problems of vedic accentuation in his work on the intonation patterns of the language of the *Taittirīya Brāhmaṇa.*[19]

## 0:3 The Western Approach

### 0.3.1 The Western Approach to *samāsa*

Brugmann[20] says that "all the developments of language noted by the terms 'stem formation' and 'inflexion' are based upon one common principle, the juxtaposition and more or less intimate fusion of elements which were originally independent." He maintains that what one says by the stem or *prātipadika* and the suffix or *pratyaya* were originally independent entities by what he calls the root period. Later, they fused to form a word and word composition was brought about. Regarding compound formation, the treatment is the same as word composition. Thus, a compound is formed by juxtaposition of independent grammatical entities.

*P* on the other hand is said to start with the obligatory status of the *pratyaya'*, the base the *prakṛti* and the *pratyaya* are irrevocably interconnected. Patañjali comments on *A* 1.2.45 (vārttika 8)

प्रत्ययेन नित्यसबन्धात्। नित्यसबन्धावतावर्थौ प्रकृतिः प्रत्यय इति । प्रत्ययेन नित्यसंबन्धात् केवलस्य प्रयोगो न भविष्यति ॥

M.D. Pandit points out that though the symbolic representations of the two views would reduce to a similar equation, the approach adopted by *P* and Brugmann are contrastive.[21]

However, the primary scholar who brought to light the work on compounds was T. Benfey who gave the designations copulative *(dvandva)*, determinative *(tatpuruṣa, karmadhāraya* and *dvigu)*, relative *(bahuvrīhi)*, inflexible *(avyayībhāva)* and the repeated formations *(āmreḍita)*.[22] Benfey is of the opinion that syntactical composition can be transformed into a compound word. Thus, Benfey followed *P* in the assumption of the origin of compound word form even from subordinate sentences.

Bopp contrarily emphasized the views of Bopadeva on the classification of compounds. His classification involves six compound types the *dvandva, bahuvrīhi, karmadhāraya, tatpuruṣa, dvigu* and *avyayībhāva,*[23] His model was adopted in the main by Max Müller.[24]

Whitney however divided Sanskrit compounds into three main classes the composite, the determinative composite and secondary adjective composite.[25] He mentions the likelihood of a genetic study of compound words. J. Speijer noticed the relations between word - formation and syntactical arrangement dividing the compounds into three major groups -

*dvandva, tatpuruṣa and bahuvrīhi.*[26] His approach has been criticised to be non-historical (M.D. Pandit, 1969)[27]. The formal exposition of compound formation belongs to Wackernagel.[28] His approach is said to deviate from the works of the traditional and offers original classifications to the problem of compounds. His approach is purely formal in stark contrast to Brugmann's semantic approach in the words of M.D. Pandit.[29]

Renou faithfully represents the Indian school of grammar but makes no attempt to study compound words independently.[30] Certain later studies include those of Roland who aims at a linguistic description of the nominal compounds from a strictly synchronic and a formal point of view, by opposing them to the respective semantically analyzed forms. Roland distinguishes between the contentive (lexical aspects) and the functors (the grammatical aspect) of a compound term.[31]

Burrow makes the observations that compound words used as adjectives are found more frequently than as nouns.[32]

It is of relevance to this thesis to refer to Al-George's work on negative compounds, the accentuation of which is highlighted briefly in Chapter 7.[33] Certain other critical works on the compound word formation include Staal,[34] Mahavira,[35] Mayrhofer[36] and Dash.[37]

### 0.3.2 Reviews of Accentuation

M.D. Balasubrahmaniam classifies the Western approach to accentuation in the following way :

1. Comparative accentuation of IE languages.
2. Descriptive studies on vedic accentuation.
3. Nature of vedic accent and vedic recitation.
4. Pāṇini and the vedic language.

This system of classification has been followed as it is useful as well as accurate.

### 0.3.2.1 Comparative Accentuation of IE Languages.

The principal authors on the scholarship of accentuation are Benloew (1847), Bopp (1854) Hankiewicz (1875) Bally (1908) and Hirt (1929).[38]

A criticism of Bopp was done by Whitney on accentuation. Bloomfield atter twenty years pointed out three fundamental principles governing IE accentuation.

First, that the IE word-accent was free and unaffected by quantity; second, the IE knew well-defined laws of sentence-accentuation; and third that the change of original accentuation was due to phonetic and analogical factors." (quoted from M.D. Balasubrahmaniam's thesis).

The accentuation of preverbs (1907) and that of IE nouns (1916) was done by Meillet.[39] Schmitt expressed a different view on the relation of accent to ablaut.[40]

Critical to the understanding of IE accentuation is the work of Kurylowicz who laid stress on the morphological role played by accent.[41]

### 0.3.2.2 Descriptive Studies on Vedic Accentuation.

Böhtlingk, Aufrecht and Whitney were principal scholars who contributed to the main facts of Sanskrit accent.[42] W.S. Allen cites correspondence between prosody and retroflexion.[43] The study of the accentuation of compounds attracted the concentrated attention of German philologists such as Garbe (1877),[44] Knauer[45] (on accentuation of negative compounds in 1885) and Reuter[46] (on the determinative compounds in 1891).

Kirfel (1908) contributed to the history of nominal composition in *Upaniṣad-s* and the Epics.

### 0.3.2.3 Nature of Vedic Accent and Vedic Recitation

It is generally believed that Haug may have been the first Westerner to hear an actual vedic recitation. Some of the later day Indologists who concentrated on vedic accent were Roth (1919), Hoogt (1929), Bake (1935) Poucha (1943)[48].

Gray carried out an extensive analysis of the Ṛgvedic

recitation.[49] Staal in 1961 arrived at the conclusion that the accent of the vedic was stress accent and not pitch accent.[50]

More recently, G. Cardona (1993) was responsible for the description of the Bhāṣikā accentuation system. Renou was responsible for focusing attention on the vedic recitation in Sanskrit and Indian Culture.[51]

#### 0.3.2.4 Pāṇini and Vedic Language

Macdonnell provided a preliminary and authoritative treatise on grammar in 1910 in his "Vedic Grammar".[52] The most important treatise in comparative grammar was made by Jakob Wackeranagel in the *"Altindische Grammatik.*[53]

Thieme explicitly felt that *P* referred to the language of the sacred texts of the *Veda.* The criticisms leveled by Whitney were rebutted by Böhthlingk.

It will be profitable to repeat here the conclusions of Thieme.

(a) Pāṇini draws his vedic sources from first hand experience.

(b) He had a precise knowledge of the *samhitā* texts *ṚV., Mais, Kāṭhas, TS, AV* the *SV.*[54]

(c) *P,* the North grammarian does not draw from the *White Yajur Veda* which is an eastern text.

(d) The best understood formulation of a vedic rule of *P* helps us to restore the reading of a text, if the vedic mss contains dubious readings.

### 0.4 The Linguistic Approach

No review on accent would be complete without making mention of Dwight Bolinger's contribution to the field of intonation in linguistics. Although he dealt primarily with the stress accent of English, his linguistic- observations on the ambiguities of pitch accent make interesting and purposive reading.[53]

Bolinger provided a comprehensive "Theory of Pitch Accent".[56] He does differentiate between the phonemic contrasts of pitch accent in languages (as Sanskrit) and the role of pitch in English where the function is not contrastive. However, in the formulation of this theory in the article he does underline and emphasize the function of pitch as segmental phonemes.

In a more detailed examination of the function of intonation, Bolinger reviews "the attempts to identify holistic lexical functions" of the same.[57] The sentence accent, the contour and contradiction are dealt here and he also draws the difference between stress (which belongs to the lexicon) and accent which belongs to the utterance.[58]

The initial studies on intonation were done by Pike.[59] Trager, Smith and Wells followed these studies with specific reference to the position of paralinguistics in the area of Linguistics and the pitch phonemes in English.[60] The assumption that phonological structures coincide one to one with deep structures is disputed by Stockwell who himself supported the view in 1960.[61] Clearly, he says there are "several kinds of correlation between deep structure and intonation but nothing is as simple as (1-1) ("*a one to one correspondence*", my emphasis). On the other hand, neither is intonation a simple fraction of surface structure as was assumed by Chomsky & Halle (1968).[62]

Here, it is worth mentioning the antecedent works of Chomsky on intonation in Modern Linguistics. His two key contributions were "The Sound Pattern of English" with Halle. M (1968) and "On accent and juncture in English" in M. Halle (ed) for Roman Jakobson, Mouton and with Linkoff. F (1956).[63]

Critical reviews and articles contributing to the area of stress include an extensive review by Joan Bresnan.[64] Selkirk draws the syntactic correspondence to stress in the English language.[65] Gregory Guy and Julia von Wilier provide the meaning of intonation in English.[66] Hadding-Koch conducted experimental studies on intonation contours.[67] The relation between intonation and grammar was pursued by Halliday.[68] The relation between meaning and speech acts was reviewed by Harnish who provided demonstration for it.[69] Subrahmanyam deals with accentuation rules in his Pāṇinian Linguistics[70] while his earlier article relates surface structure to deep structure in *P*.[71]

Ladd elaborated the details of the structure of intonational meaning.[72] Reviews on suprasegementals and intonation have been carried out by Lahiste,[71] Liberman[74] and Lieberman[75] the latter relating it to perception as well. Newman[76] restricts his paper to the stress system of English while colloquial English comes under review in O'Connor.[77]

A recent overview of accent among different languages of the world was provided by Alan Cruttendon.[78]

With specific reference to vedic accent, Kiparsky has followed a model of sentence accentuation which he delineates in detail, with specific correlation to Pāṇinian accentual rules though he dismisses the complete authority of the commentarial tradition vis-à-vis accentual rules.[79-80]

A recent systematic introduction of P's accentual rules is provided by G. Cardona[81] who gives an adequately sufficient description for the '*satiśiṣṭa*' principle, so crucial to the devolution of accent.

## REFERENCES

1. Balasubrahinaniam M.D., 1981.
2. Ibid., Chapter 1.
3. Abhyankar, T.B., 1946.
4. Devasthali, G.V., 1983.
5. Sastri, Sivaramakrishna, 1936.
6. Abhyankar, K.V., 1896.
7. Bhattacarya, Vidusekhara, 1944.
8. Varma, Siddeswar, 1951.
9. Murti, Srimannarayana, 1974.
10. Roland, Harweg, 1964.
11. Raja Kunhan, 1928.
12. Sankaran, C.R., 1935.
13. Sehgal, S.R., 1941.

14. Balasubrahmaniam, M.D., 1981.
15. Laddu, S.D., 1969.
16. Bh-Svara here in this quotation refers to *Bhāṣā-Svara*.
17. Varma, Siddheswar, 1951.
18. Varma, Siddheswar, 1945.
19. Ananthanarayana, H.S., 1971
20. Brugmann, Karl,1891.
21. Pandit, M.D., 1989.
22. Benfey, Th., 1862.
23. Bopp, F., 1845.
24. Mueller, Max, 1866.
25. Whitney, W.D., 1861.
26. Speijer, J., 1896.
27. Pandit, M.D., 1969.
28. Wackernagel, Jakob, 1905.
29. Pandit, M.D., 1969.
30. Renou, L., 1936.
31. Roland, Harweg, 1964.
32. Burrow, T.,1959.
33. Al-George, Sergin, 1983.
34. Staal, F., 1966.
35. Mahavira, 1972.
36. Mayrhofer, M.A., 1978.
37. Dash, S., 1992.
38. cited from Balasubrahmaniam, M.D., 1981.
39. Meillet, 1934.
40. Schmitt, 1953.
41. Kurylowicz, J.,1958.
42. Böhtlingk, Otto, 1848.
43. Allen, W.S.,1959.

44-48 cited from Balasubrahmaniam M.D., 1981.

49. Gray, J.E.B., 1959.
50. Staal, F., 1966.
51. Renou, L., 1950.
52. Macdonnell, 1910.
53. Wackernagel, Jakob, 1910.
54. Ṛg-Veda, Maitrāyaṇi Saṁhitā-s, Kāṭhaka Saṁhitā-s, Taittirīya Saṁhitā-s, AtharvaVeda.
55. Bolinger, Dwight, 1961 b.
56. Bolinger, Dwight, 1958,
57. Bolinger, Dwight, 1978,
58. Bolinger, Dwight, 1961 a.
59. Pike, K.L., 1945.
60. cited in Bolinger, 1961b.
61. Stockwell, Robert, 1972.

62. Chomsky Noam and Halle, Morris. 1968.
63. Chomsky Noam and Linkoff F., 1956.
64. Bresnan, Joan, 1971.
65. Selkirk, Elizabeth, 1980 b.
66. Guy Gregory and von Wilier, Julia, 1984.
67. Hadding - Koch et al., 1964.
68. Halliday, 1967 a.
69. Harnish, Robert, M., 1977 a.
70. Subrahmanyam P.S., 1999.
71. Subrahmanyam, P.S., 1972.
72. Ladd, Robert, D., 1980.
73. Lehiste, Ilse, 1970.
74. Liberman, Mark et al, 1977.
75. Lieberman, Philip, 1967.
76. Newman, Stanley, S., 1946.
77. O'Connor, J.D., Arnold, J.F., 1961.
78. Cruttendon, Alan, 1992.
79. Kiparsky, Paul, 1982.
80. Kiparsky, Paul in *Amṛtadhāra,* Ed. S.D. Joshi, 1984.
81. Cardona, George, 1997.

*CHAPTER - 1*

# INTRODUCTION

Accent which broadly can be recognized as a suprasegmental feature falls under the study of prosodic which though peripheral to the essential features of Linguistics, forms an integral part of communication, more so verbal communication. Although, linguists like Lyons[1] contest the very notion of paralinguistic features being "peripheral" or "marginal", Lyons differentiates between verbal, prosodic, and paralinguistic components. Stress (one of the prosodic features) is abundantly seen in the English language as well as the Romance languages such as Italian (here word stress serves to distinguish cánto (I sing) from cantó (He/She sang)).

Boundaries are drawn between prosodic features and pure paralinguistic features which help define the role of each such feature with respect to semantics. "First, it would probably be agreed to by linguists that, although all the components that we have recognized are essential, the verbal component is more central than the non verbal component, and that prosodic features are more central than paralinguistic features; that within the set of prosodic features some like stress and intonation are more central than others; and that paralinguistic features are more central (or perhaps one should say less peripheral) than voice quality "(Lyons, 1993).

Crystal points out that the tendency to broaden the sense of the word 'paralinguistic has been stretched beyond function.[2] Thus the term 'paralanguistic' (though it presupposes language) can be conveniently dropped.

## 1.1 Accent *(svara)* - General Characteristics

The suprasegmentals form a crucial part of prosodic phenomena. The components of prosody include stress, accent and tone (intonation). Of these, it is the pitch-accent (the *svara),* which is musical in nature, that dominates the chant of the vedic. Even prior to P's mention and delineation of the various accents, the *Prātiśākhya-s* mention, define and elaborate on the nature of the *svara.*[3]

According to the *Prātiśākhya-s* there are the three principal *svara-s - udātta, anudātta* and *svarita.* It is *P* who gives designatory status to these *svara-s.* He defines them, borrowing from the antecedent *Prātiśākhya-s* as

उच्चैरुदात्तः (*A* 1.2.29)

नीचैः अनुदात्तः (*A* 1.2.30)

समाहारः स्वरितः (*A* 1.2.31)

The *Pāṇinīya - Śikṣā* defines them as

"उदातश्चानतुदात्तश्च स्वरितश्च स्वरास्त्रयः"

Kātyāyana mentions the subdivisions of *svarita* as

(1) *jātya*

(2) *abhinihata*

(3) *kṣaipra*

(4) *praśliṣta*

(5) *tairovyañjana*

(6) *tairovirāma*

(7) *pādavṛtta*

(8) *tathābhāvya*

Kāṇva gives one more accent the *udātta-maya*[4]

"उदात्तमयोन्यत्र नीच एव अन्तोदात्तमधयोदात्तयोः पर्वणोरन्यत्रेति कारणात् परो नीच्च उदात्तमय एव भवति प्रचित एव भवति इत्यर्थः"

Vidhata Misra makes a note of the emotional content of svara as observed in the A.[5]

Based on his observations from *A* 8.1, *A* 8.2 and *A* 6.2. Vidhata Misra concludes that the accents could have been introduced into language at a particular time as they occur naturally in daily conversation.[6]

**1.1.1 Functions of Accent.**

Some of the obvious explanations given by scholars for the need and function of accent are economy and homonymy. In both such instances context becomes axial. The outstanding illustration is that of the compound lexeme which differentiates as *bv* or *tp* depending on the position of the *svara.*[7]

The example of इन्द्रशत्रु is a common and exemplary one.

Further Misra contends that the interpretation of the *mahā vākya-s* of the *Upaniṣad-s* too rest on the relative position of *svara* on the maxims.[8]

e.g. (आत्मा) तत् त्वमसि

Some split it as आत्मा + तत् while others as आत्मा + अतत्. If अ after त् has *udātta* then splitting it as तत् is correct. Misra contends that if it is स्वरित it is अतत्.

A major function of the accent was also its pragmatic use. In a sense it *(svara)* becomes irrevocably tied to the फल (the proper & correct attainment) of the ritual. One could also see here a room for explorations of truth notions with respect to *svara.* Since *svara* is central to the process of ritualization, its pragmatic use as a truth notion too (with respect to the proper expected outcome of the ritual) is important.

The other functions by which *svara* became indispensable was by rote learning and the need to construct a '*pada-pāṭha*'. It is also interesting to note what the *mīmamsakā-s* have to say.[9]

**( तेनादृष्टार्थ एवायं स्वरपाठोऽवगम्यते। सर्वदा ब्रह्मयज्ञाङ्ग द्रव्ययज्ञजपेषु च,** *Tantravārttika,* 1.3.9)

Accent is also said to complement the presence of *mantras* during the chant of the *Veda-s*. Together they constitute a meaningful performance of ritual.

### 1.1.2 The Nature of Accent

In the introduction to *Svarasiddhāntacandrikā,* Śiva-ramakrishna Sastri,[10] comments on the relative difference of the three accents in the following words.

"According to Indian tradition the three accents are pronounced thus, *udātta* in a middle tone, *svarita* in a high tone and *anudātta* in a low tone. This practice is prevalent today throughout India in the recitation of the *Veda-s* with three accents. The peculiarities of each recension of a *Veda* are known; one syllable is uttered in one recension in the *udātta* accent, as in the *Vājasaneya Brāhmaṇa.* This change cannot be effected by the student of the *Veda-s* of his own accord but only with the authority of the relevant *Prātiśakhya-s* and other works on accent. A similar practice is found regarding *anudātta* and *svarita* but never is *udātta* pronounced in a low tone or *svarita* in a middle tone".

Wackernagel says *"udātta* is really the high tone, being so literally as well as by the definition as given by *P* a vowel spoken with high tone is called *udātta"* According to the authors of the *Prātiśākhya-s* the production of distinct tones was intimately connected to the production of air and breath control.[11]

This theory of the antecedent *Prātiśākhya* authors is disputed by Patañjali as the definition does not give a fixed standard of determining the high and the low (tone).

#### 1.1.2.1 Representations of Accent

According to *Vidhata Misra* on the commentary on the *Pratijñā sūtra* the symbolic representation of a particular accent is made by a movement of the hand.[12] "Thus in the low accent, the right hand is to be placed or moved near the heart; in articulating the high accent, the hand is to be near the head; while in the case of *svarita* the hand is to be near the ear. The movement of the hand in the direction of the head, the heart and the ear are symbolic..............."

Yet the fact that Patañjalī and Nāgeśa attribute the high accent to the higher part of the vocal organs coming in contact with breath, ndicates that the element of breath-force is not entirely excluded from the view of accent But the predominance of the musical accent is quite plain

**1.1.3 Accent Marking**

Every word in the *Ṛg Veda*(*RV*) is marked with an accent Each word carries an accent. Compounds too exhibit this property of a unitary accent with the exception of a few illustrations such as *Bṛhaspati* which have two accents.

Accentuation is seen as marking in some manuscripts of the old literature, namely in the primary vedic texts or *Saṁhitā-s* in two of the *Brāhmaṇa-s* (*Taittirīya* and *Śatapatha* and the *Taittirīya Āraṇyaka* and in the *Suparṇādhyāya*

The standard mode of marking is to use a vertical bar on top of the syllable carrying the *udātta,*

According to Macdonell in the *RV* the pitch of the *udātta* is intermediate between the other two tones. Thus in *RV* the *udātta* is not marked as the principal accent. The preceding *anudātta* is indicated below the syllable bearing it by a horizontal stroke, while the following *svarita,* which rises to a higher pitch is indicated by a vertical bar above the syllable carrying it.

The *Maitrāyani Saṁhitā* on the other hand indicates the independent *svarita* by a curve below

The dependent *svarita* is indicated by a horizontal stroke crossing the middle of the syllable or by the vertical strokes above it.

In the Sāmaveda the numerals (1,2,3 1,2,3) are written above the accented syllable to mark the *udātta,* the *svarita* and the *anudātta* respectively as representing three degrees of pitch

The numeral 2 is used to indicate *udātta* when there is no following *svarita.*

When two *udātta-s* follow each other, the latter is not marked And, an independant *svarita* is marked by 2

The *Śatapatha Brāhmaṇa* marks the *udātta* only.[14]

**1.1.4 Lack of Accent**

Accent loss can be due to the nature of particles.[15]

(1) Among the first category are

(i) Pronouns

*ena* (he, she, it)

*tva* (another) *sama* (some)

(ii) Personal pronouns of first and second persons

*mā*

*tvā*

*me*

*te*

*nau*

*vām*

*nas*

*vas*

(iii) Forms of demonstrative stems 'i' and 'sa'

*im*

*sim*

(2) Loss due to syntactical position

(i) vocatives unless in the beginning of a sentence or *pada*

(ii) finite verbs in principal clauses unless beginning the sentence.

(iii) oblique cases of the pronoun 'a', if unemphatic and not beginning the sentence or *pada.*

e.g. *asya janmāni (his births),*

but *āsyā uṣāsaḥ* (of that dawn)

(iv) *yathā* invariably in the sense of *iva* 'like', it occurs at the end of a pada e.g. *tāyāvs yathā,* 'like thieves'.

### 1.1.5 Accent Terminology

To clearly understand the concordance between the Western and Indian Terminology of the accent in a word, refer M.D.Balasubrahmaniam (1981)[16]. If by *anudāttam padam ekavarjam (A* 6.1.158) the only accent of a word is *udātta* then according to its position it is said to be ādyudātta (initial acute) or *antodātta* (final actue) or middle acute madhyodātta. These correspond to barytone, oxytone and paroxytone designations respectively.

/ \ \ \. = barytone _ / _ _ = Proparoxytone

\ \ \ / = oxytone \ \ / \ = Paroxytone

The rising tone is denoted by ( / )

M.D. Balasubrahmaniam gives the example of the compound *āmalakījah* where a sequence of four steps may occur :

(i) initial affix accent by *(ṅīṣaḥ pratyaya- ādyudāttatvam)*

(ii) *kṛt* accent *(gatikāraka-upapadāt kṛt A* 6.2.139, *kṛt* accent)

(iii) baroxytonisation of initial accent by *dīrgha kāśa tuṣ a bhrāṣṭra-vaṭaṁ A* 6.2.82 *(pūrvapada ādyudātta)*

(iv) proparoxytonisation by *antyāt pūrvam bahv acaḥ A* 6.2.83 *iti - lakāra - akārasya udāttatvam.*

### 1.1.6 Unitary accent in a Word

The accent of a compound is generally governed by *samāsasya (A* 6.1.223) which ordains a final acute on the compound. The necessity of prescribing this *antodātta* arises due to a need to discern between the ordainment of *pratyaya-svara (ādyudāttaś ca, A* 3.1.3), *dhātu-svara (dhātoḥ, A* 6.1.162) which are prescribed in sections prior to the sections dealing with accentuation of compounds.

The exceptions such as the disyllabic nature of some of the *dvandva* compounds and the exception to the *antodātta* are dealt with in respect to *dvigu, bahuvrīhi* and *pūrvapada-prakṛtisvara* of certain *tatpuruṣa,* conditioned by semantic conditions, stated in those specific *sūtra-s*. But it is imperative to examine the importance of the *sūtra-s* dealing with the accentuation of suffixes, which in *samāsa* formation contribute to the devolution of the unitary accent of the compound. Besides, in those sections of this thesis dealing with *kṛt* accent and *samāsāntodātta* (of a compound) there is a dire need to understand at least perfunctorily the accent of the suffix.

As the nature of *pratyayasvara* has already been dealt with by M.D. Balasubrahmaniam in his work on *kṛt* suffixation and accentuation, it is appropriate here to offer only an introduction to the topic to get a feel of work previously done.

Begging P's description of these suffixes is whether apart from the function of dropping the *anubandha* at the end of the suffixes, do these '*pratyayasvara-s* (as ordained by *ādyudāttaś ca A 3.1.3)* have any real function at all. In addressing these primary and fundamental concerns, M.D. Balasubrahmaniam has gone on to build a thesis on the regularity of *kṛt* suffixation and accentuation. What seemed irrelevant or ambiguous at the level of a suffix was demonstrated to be essential in word formation and word-accentuation.

### 1.1.6.1 *pratyayasvara*

The general rule आद्युदात्तश्च *ādyudāttaś ca* (A 3.1.3) is

the *sūtra* governing the accent of an affix - the *pratyaya-svara* which is regarded to be acute - initial on the *pratyaya*. But there are specific exceptions to this generalisation.

Typically, the indicatory *IT* of the *anubandha* governs the final acute in these instances of exceptions. The interdependence of accent on *IT* characters is discussed with specific reference to *samāsānta* suffixation and accent in Chapter 2.7 but it would be useful to look at these particular exceptions to *ādyudātta* in certain *pratyaya-s*. In examining these exceptions we can come to appreciate the relevance of dealing with accent and *anubandha*

**1.1.6.1.A The Default Operation**

The affix तव्य has *udātta* on the first अ and thus we get a form as कर्त्तव्यम् This is the default operation of most *pratyayasvaras*.

**1.1.6.1.B The Exceptions**

Most of the exceptions are specified by *sūtra-s* in section *A* 6.1 dealing with accentuation of affixes.

*A* 6.1.163[18]

affixes with indicatory च will have *udātta* on the final.

*A* 6.1.217[19]

affixes with indicatory र have accent in the penultimate position of a polysyllabic.

*A* 6.1.193[20]

those having indicatory ल throw acute accent on syllable immediately preceding the affix.

*A* 6.1.197[21]

affix with indicatory ञ and न have accute on the first syllable of the word to which they are added.

*A* 6.1.165[22]

*taddhita* affix with indicatory क takes acute accent on the final.

*A* 6.1.185[23]

affix having as indicatory त is *svarita*.

*A 3.1.4* [24]

affix with indicatory प is *anudātta*.

In looking at these exceptions it becomes clear that the *anubandha* or indicatory *IT* is of primary importance in determining the type of accent and the position (acute - initial or actue - final) of the *svara* in the *pratyaya*. It is important to take note of the fact that the *IT* of the *pratyayasvara* having indicatory च or a base with indicatory च (*A* 6.1.163) ultimately fix the accent on the same syllable of the word in certain instances.

### 1.1.6.3 *āgamasvara*

e.g. चत्वारि :

### 1.1.6.4 *dhātusvara*

The *sūtra,* धातोः *dhātoḥ* (*A* 6.1.162) enjoins an *antodātta* for the verbal root. There are however also observations made by *P* on the peculiarity by which certain endings of the root take particular aspects.

## 1.2 Accent in Compounds

### 1.2.1 *tp* Accent

*tp-s* exhibit the final acute (अन्तोदात्त) on the compound as ordained in समासस्य *samāsaya(A* 6.1.223). Certain semantic conditions impose a *pūrvapadaprakṛtisvara* in exceptions. The relationship of *samāsānta* to *antodātta* and the exceptions are discussed in Chapter 3 of this thesis under the details of the *sūtra, samāsasya* समासस्य (*A* 6.1.223).

e.g. *Uda-meghá* (shower of water ) when second member is an agent noun.

### 1.2.2 *bv* Accent

*bv* -s are governed by *bahivrīhau prakṛtyā pūrvapadam* (A 6.2.1) which is an *apavāda* to *A* 6.1.223 and therefore retains *pūrvapadaprakṛtisvara*. The nature of this rule is discussed in Chapter 3.

e.g. *viśváto-mukha,* (facing in all directions).

Here only a short introduction to the nature of accent of these two types is provided as a prelude to detailing certain comments in the *Mbh* regarding *svara, samāsānta* and *liṅga.*

### 1.2.3 Comment from the *Samarthāhnika*

The entire *Mbh* on *samartha padavidhi A* 2.1.1 deals with the various aspects of semantic fitness in word-formation (with respect of course only to certain types of finished words).

Compounds form a critical discussion in these. In dealing with the formation of two membered and later in the discussion of three membered compounds, the resolution of meaning, given the word order and compounding is made clear. For example, S.D. Joshi (1979) has explained the difference in splitting up a three membered compound by right hand or left hand analysis. In his interpretation of Kaiyaṭa's resolution of the compound "*mahākaṣṭaṁśritaḥ*" he goes to elaborate in detail as to why only one of those analyses is possible. At the end, the discussion of many-membered *samāsasvara* accent crops up again, this time to determine the desired accentuation.

In what seems more like a dialectic tailored to create a theory for P's rules than an observation of fact, there is a tremendous impetus to explain away the nature of accent in three (or more) - membered compounds. It is worthwhile to keep in mind that the usages in the Veda were diverse and there still remains much doubt if P's rules can completely account for these usages. (M.D.Balasubrahmaniam, 1981.)[25]

Hence Patañjali takes up specific examples and tries to highlight the problems in accentuation and compound word formation. One of the factors underpinning accentuation is whether the internal construction is *tp* or *bv*. For example if a compound is ABC, AB could well be a *tp* or *bv* and ABC a *tp* or *bv* depending on semantic fitness. Given this complexity how will one account for the accent of the internal compound in relation to the accent of the three membered compound. The question naturally here is "Which of these *svara-s* takes precedence?"

The *vārttika* 29 deals with these problems. Patañjali takes up the examples *pūrvaśālāpriyaḥ, adhikaṣaṣṭhivarṣaḥ* and *ekaśitipād*. Here we make an attempt to highlight the complexity of accentuation using the illustrations, detailing each, one by one.

The necessity to discuss the problem of accent in many-membered compounds is addressed primarily in the backdrop of determining the number of words that can go to form a *bv* (*vārttika* 28)[26]. In Patañjali's explanation one finds that compounding many words is a likely possibility but with certain difficulties.

*vārttika* 29

**तत्र स्वरसमासान्तपुंवद्भावेषु दोषः**

Kātyāyana clearly observes that the accent change at the end of a compound and treatment of feminine form as masculine are difficulties to be explained in many membered compounding. It is clear from these revelatory *vārttika-s* of Kātyāyana that the vedic usages would have been diverse and *P's* rules are not an accurate reflection of the usage *per se*. This leads one to dwell on the rationalizations on accent rules and possibilities, whether a rule governed phonemic system can account for accent.

### 1.2.3.1 *pūrvaśālāpriyaḥ, adhikasaṣṭhivarṣaḥ* and *ekaśitipād* e.g. 1 *pūrvaśālāpriyaḥ*

This is a *bv*, *pūrvaśālāpriyaḥ* dissolving as *pūrvaśālā priyā yasya*. Due to the effect of A 2.1.51[27] the *bv* becomes the condition for the *tp* construction; *tp* is therefore the *nimittin* (the conditioned form); *bv svara* the *nimittasvara* and *tp svara* the *nimittisvara*.

The *nimittisvara* is the *udātta* on the *tp* construction and this comes only after the *bv* accent.

Whether the accent of the internal *tp* prevails over the *bv* accent is the discussion attempted in the *Mbh*. Only one accent can prevail in a compound as stated in *anudāttam padam ekavarjam* (*A* 6.1.158), however many members there are to a compound. In forming a compound as *pūrvaśālāpriyaḥ* there 'seems' to be a conflict between the operations of *A* 6.1.223 and *A* 6.2.1 which govern *tp* and *bv* accentuation. The intricacies of these *sūtra-s* are dealt with in Chapter 3. S.D. Joshi points out that although an *apavāda* rule (*A* 6.2.1) can prevail over *antaraṅga* (*A* 6.1.223) according to *paribhāṣā* 38[28] he shows that the grammatical sequences in which the operation of *tp* occurs after *bv* formation are distinct. The *tp* accent is thus delinked from *bv* accent. Since the domains of operations of these two grammatical sequences- *bv* construction followed by *tp* formation- are distinct, there is no real conflict of interest. Therefore *samāsasya*(*A* 6.1.223) the *antaraṅga* supercedes *A* 6.2.1. (*paribhāṣā* 50)[29]

But this still does not explain how *pūrvaśālāpriyaḥ* obtains *bv* accent. To elaborate on this Patañjali makes the definition of *nimitti* and *nimittasvara* while commenting on *vārttika-32*[20]. The need to define accent as *nimittisvara* or *nimittasvara* arises as none of the general modes of operation of *sūtra-s* explain the precedence the *bv svara* takes over *tp* accent although the relation between the two *sūtra-s* in question is *bahiraṅga* and *antaraṅga*. The *satiśiṣṭa* principle also does not apply here. It is only in redefining *tp* (internal) *svara* and *bv svara* as *nimittisvara* and *nimittasvara* that a resolution of accent is seen in *pūrvaśālāpriyaḥ*.

### 1.2.3.2 e.g.2 *ekáśitipād*

However, in examples such as *ekaśtipād,* the *tp nimitti-svara* takes precedence over the *nimttasvara*. This poses the question whether a separate rule should be made to accomodate this seeming anamoly. Kātyāyana pithily phrases his *vārttika*.

*vārttika* 33

एकशितिपात्स्वरवचनं तु ज्ञापकं
निमित्तिस्वरबलीयस्त्वस्य ।

Patañjali explains that in such examples as mentioned by

Kātyāyana (i.e. *ekaśtipād)* the accent of the internal *tp ekaśiti* prevails over the conditioning form. Kaiyaṭa provides the elaboration that when one deals with a *tripadabahuvrīhi* and when the internal *tp* follows, then the compound has *udātta* on the first syllable and that this is established by *bahuvrīhau prakṛtyā pūrvapadam(A* 6.2.1).

In the case that two different accent rules apply, as per *vārttika* 33, the accent of conditional form *ekaśiti* prevails over accent of *ekaśitipād.*

The Translator S.D. Joshi shows three possibilities.

1. If the word is considered as a *tripadabahuvrīhi,* then the internal construction is a *tp.* If the *vārttika* 33 prevails the compound takes on *dvigu* accentuation. Here, S.D. Joshi points out that whether or not one accepts this clue, does not make a difference in the accentuation.
2. If the *tp* is first formed as *ekaśitīḥ* and then the *bv* as *ekaśitipād* then subsequently the *bv* that is formed will still have *udātta* on the first syllable *(A* 6.2.1).
3. If the inside construction is *bv (eka śitir eṣu)* then the accent falls on the first member of inside *bv* by *A* 6.2.1. This accent is not changed when, afterwards, we form the compound as a *bv.*

Hence in all three possibilities the accent will fall on the first syllable of *ekaśitipād.*

1. Kātyāyana formulates *vārttikanimittisvarabalīsya-stvāt vā.*
2. Then, he rejects his own *vārttika* by saying he can justify the desired accent by taking a clue from P's procedure.
3. Patañjali rejects this because the word *ekaśitipād* cannot give us a clue.

And therefore, a special rule is required.

### 1.2.3.3 e.g.3 *adhikasaṣṭhivarṣaḥ*

The argument is as follows - the consideration of *adhikasaṣṭhivarṣaḥ* is the generalization of *tripadabahuvrīhi* and aids in elimination of the undesirable forms such as *adhikaśatavarṣa.*

In considering whether this is to be interpreted as "having more than a hundred years" or "having one hundred years more". The interpreter[31] says *adhikaśatavarṣa* is not desired and one derives *adhikaśatavarṣa* according to A 6.2.1. But it is pointed out in *Mbh* that in *adhikaṣaṣṭhivarṣa* also *samāsānta* is taken up as per the specification of Kātyāyana.

*nistrimśat* + Ḍac - *nistrimśa* (A 6.4.143)

Similarly, the internal construction of *adhikaṣaṣṭhi* will be *tp* by A 2.1.51. Since it ends in a numeral by the *vārttika adhikaṣaṣṭhi* will take *ḍac.*

But the translator shows how *bv* can also apply by the rule *bahuvrīhau saṁkhyeye ḍac abahugaṇāt* (A 5.4.73). To resolve this only by accentuation the possible options are

A. *adhikaṣaṣṭhivarṣa* as a *bv* with internal *tp.*

B. *adhikaṣaṣṭhivarṣa* as a *bv* within a *bv*

C. A *bv* of 3 words

D. Obviate Ḍac which gives *adhikaśata varṣa* and form an internal *tp* - *dvigu* construction.

With respect to the *"adhikaṣaṣṭhivarṣa"* two possibilities of meaning - analysis are :

1. *adhikā ṣaṣṭhi varṣāṇi yasya (ṣaṣṭhi* represents object numeral)

2. *adhikā ṣaṣṭhi varṣāṇām asya* where *ṣaṣṭhi varṣāṇām* stands in genitive relation as *ṣaṣṭhi* represents number only.

The question then is ... "What does the word *ṣaṣṭhi* in the compound represent - number *(saṁkhyā)* or object connected with number *(saṁkhyeya)*".

It is possible to construct a *tripadabahuvrīhi* and have the desired form *adhikaṣaṣṭhivarṣa* without intervention by *Ḍac*, the *samāsānta*. Kaiyaṭa points out that *adhikaśatavarṣah* cannot be a *tp* according to *taddhitārthottarapada (samāhāre ca)*. Then the internal compound will have *udātta* on the last syllable whereas *udātta* on the first syllable is desired.

According to him even if the internal *dvigu* gives the result in *adhikaṣaṣṭhivarṣa* it will not do so in *adhikasatavarṣa*. In this form the final syllable of the internal construction will be accentuated *(adhikasatā)* by *A* 6.1.223. Here *A* 6.2.29 cannot over rule *A* 6.1.223 because the numeral *śata* does not end in '*ik*' Therefore to prevent the undesired accent by *A* 6.1.223 a special provision is necessary, to list this word in the '*yuktarohin*' list.

Thus *dvandva bv* can have as many components as possible *(Bahuvrīhidvandvāhnika, 1974)*.

### 1.2.3.4 Force of *sūtra-s A* 6.1.223, *A* 6.2.1 from *Paribhāṣenduśekhara*

Accentuation of the last syllable of the internal this case the accentuation based on the *tp* construction is *antaraṅga*. Therefore it prevails over the accent based on *bahuvrīhi* construction which is *bahiraṅga*. This is reflected by *paribhāṣ ā* L (50) in the *Paribhāṣenduśekara*: .

An operation or a rule becomes *antaraṅga* when a sequence of grammatical units governed by the rule is required by another operation or rule *(bahiraṅga)*. The *tp* accentuation requires the sequence AB, whereas the *bv* requires the sequence ABC.

## 1.3 Comment from the *Vākyapadīya*

Helarāja takes up the analysis of the compound '*mahākaṣ taṁśritaḥ*' and comments on the *svarabheda* of the different forms obtained. He points out that in the two membered compound by अहीने द्वितीया *(A* 6.2.48) one obtains *pūrvapadaprakṛtisvara* and the अवयव (or internal construction) gets *samāsāntodātta*.[34]

Helarāja also points out that in the example महाराण्यम् it retains the accent of internal *tp*; (two membered) that dominates in the compound, due to the '*thāthā-svara*' and not due to *samāsāntodātta* which is contradicted.[35]

Helarāja explains that *svara* is due to the principle of *satiśiṣ ṭa* due to which the *antodātta* comes about.[36] He explains the possibility of doṣa if *madhyodātta* comes in the three membered compound and *antodātta* in the internal *tp*. In his words this is resolved not merely by the rule '*saha-supā*' (*A* 1.1.3) which makes allowance for multi-membered compounding but due to a lack of contradiction in accent.

"तथा च सुप् सुपेति संख्या विवक्षायां त्रिपदसमासः न भवति। महाकष्टश्रिते तु स्वरभेदाभावात् सत्यपि त्रिपदे समासे नास्ति कश्चिद् दोषः।" (*Helarāja* on VP).[38]

## REFERENCES


1. Lyons, John, 1993.
2. Crystal, David, 1969.
3. Mishra, Vidhata, 1972.
4. Ibid.
5. Ibid.
6. Ibid.
7. K.V. Abhyankar, J.M. Shukla, Paspaśāhnika, 1968.
8. Mishra, Vidhata, 1972.
9. Ibid.
10. Sastri, K.A. Sivaramakrishna, 1936.
11. Wackernagal, Jakob, 1910.
12. Mishra, Vidhata, 1972.
13. Ibid.
14. Ibid.
15. Ibid.
16. Balasubrahmaniam, M.D., 1981.
17. Ibid.
18. चित्तः (A 6.1.163). A stem haring indicatory च् gets acute on end syllable (Trans., S.C. Vasu, 1997).
19. उपोत्तमः रिति (A 6.1.217)

    What is formed by an affix having an imdicatory र् has acute on the penultimate syllable. (Trans., S.C. Vasu, 1997)
20. लिति (A 6.1.193)

The acute accent falls on the syllable immediately preceding the affix that has imdicatory ल् ()Trans., S.C. Vasu, 1997)

21. ञ्नित्यादिर्नित्यम् (A 6.1.1997)

 Whatever is derived with an affix having an indicatory ञ् or न् have acute accent invariably on the first syllable. (Trans., S.C Vasu, 1997)

22. कित: (A 6.1.165)

 A stem formed by a taddhita affix having an indicatory क has acute final on end syllablle. (Trans., S.C. Vasu, 1997)

23. तित्वरितम् (A 6.1.165)

 An affix having indicatory त् is *svarita i.e.* has circumflex accent. (Trans., S.C. Vasu, 1997)

24. अनुदात्तौ सुप्पितौ (A 3.1.4)

 The case affixes सुप् an case affix having पित् are *anudātta.* (Trans., S.C. Vasu, 1997)

25. Balasubrahmaniam, M.D., 1981
26. *Vārttika* 28

 अविशेषण बहुव्रीहावनेकपदप्रसङ्गः।

27. तद्धितार्थोत्तरपदसमाहारे च (A 2.1.51)
28. *Paribhāṣenduśekhara, paribhāṣā* 38

 पूर्वपरनित्यान्तरङ्गापवादानामुत्तरोत्तरं।

29. *Paribhāṣenduśekhara, paribhāṣā* 50

 असिद्धं बहिरङ्गमन्तरङ्गे।

30. *Vārttika* 32 निमित्तिस्वरबलीयस्त्वाद्वा।
31. Joshi, S. D., *Samarthāhnika,* 1968 University of Poona, Pune.
32. "*dacaḥ prakaraṇe saṁkhyāyā tat puruṣasyopasaṁkhyānaṁ nistrimśā-dyartham.*" Joshi, S. D., *Samarthāhnika,* 1968.
33. *Paribhāṣenduśekhara, paribhāṣā* 50

 असिद्धं बहिरङ्गमन्तरङ्गे।

34. Raghunatha Sharma, 1977,

 महाकष्टश्रितेत्येवं वा स्यात् भेद: पदगये।

 वृत्तावयवस्यात्तवं यसान्न प्रतिषिध्यते।। 30।।

35. Raghunatha Sharma, 1977,

 महाराणमतीते तु त्रिपदाद् भिद्यते स्वर।

 यस्मान् तत्रान्तरङ्गत्वाद् बाधाकोऽवयवस्वर: ।।61।।

36. Ibid
37. Raghunatha Sharma, 1977,

 सतिसिष्टबलीयतस्त्वात् थाथादिस्वर एव तु।

 द्विपदे तेन युगपद् त्रितयं न समस्यते ।।62।।

38. Raghunatha Sharma, 1977, p. 68.

*CHAPTER - 2*

# SAMĀSĀNTA SUFFIXATION

## 2.1 *samāsānta* in Compound Word Formation

The *samāsānta-s* are the compositional suffixes of IE antiquity and contribute to the morphological closure of the compound. These *samāsānta-s* are more common in the *bv-s*. The suffixes most favored are *-ka, -i, -ya* and *-a*.

The suffix *-ka* is identical to the *taddhita* affix but the latter is accented while the former is not.

The compositional suffix *-i* of *bv* is distinctly of IE origin as in *prátya-ardhi* and *dhūmá-gandhi*.

The *samāsānta -ya* is seen in the original IE too.

Greek : *ennea-boios* (worth nine pieces of cattle)

Latin : *acu-ped -ius* (swift footed)

Avestan : *hapta-māh-ya*

Sanskrit : *(sapta)-mās-ya*

The commonest of all the *samāsānta-s* (and *P* deals only with this) is the compositional *-a* which goes back to the original IE. Gradually this *samāsānta -a* became so popular in Sanskrit that it often replaced the suffixal endings of second members, particularly of those ending in *-an* and *-l* (Batakrishna Ghosh, 1988).

### 2.1.1 Definition of *samāsānta*

*Samāsānta-s* are suffixes added and then elided in the final stage of the morphological process of compound word formation. They form the last section of the 5th *adhyāya* 4th *pāda* of the *A* as *taddhita* affixes devoid of sense. Otto Bohtlingk describes *samāsānta* in *samāsāntāḥ (A* 5.4.68) as "ohne die bedeutung desselben zu andern".[1] George Cardona hints at the senseless nature of the *samāsānta* in his study of bases, affixes and meaning.[2] Dipti Sharma presents the traditional classification of *samāsānta* as *atyantasvārthika pratyaya?*

### 2.1.2 Nature of *samāsānta* Suffixation

Each *samāsānta* carries an accent (carried by the *anubandha)* and contributes to the acute final *svara* of a compound.

The *samāsānta ṭac* for example acts in the following sequence in the formation of the word *'durga'*. Citing *A* 5.4.92[4] which prescribes *ṭac* when

*'go'* occurs at the end of a *tp (Avyayībvāvatatpuruṣāhnika,* 1969).

*durgo* + ṭac = *durgo* + *a*

= *durgav* + *a (A* 6.1.78)

The process of suffixation is seen to be regular in most cases; however, the endings are varied after suffixation. This property of *samāsānta* suffixes is dealt with in Chapter 2.7.

There are 92 *sūtra-s* describing the conditions for the process of *samāsānta* suffixation in *tp* and *bv*. The *sūtra*-s dealing with *samāsānta* suffixation in *tp-s* precede those of *bv* hinting at the greater complexity of *bv* accentuation.

Whether the suffixation is in *bv* or *tp, samāsānta* contributes to the finish, the designation and the morphological closure of the compound. Although every *sūtra* concerning the process of suffixation prescribes a semantic condition necessary for suffixation, arguably the most emphatic comment on the sense-less nature of this *taddhita* affix comes from a study of bases and affixes.[5]

This chapter deals primarily with the morphological

processes of *samāsānta* suffixation with a preview to introducing the function of *samāsāntāḥ (A* 5.4.68) as an *adhikāra* rule in Chapter 2.4. The considerations of a semantic basis for suffixation we appropriately felt belonged to a discussion on its relationship to accent in compounds morphological which can be more than well substantiated by the internal evidence in the *A* and the Pāṇinian commentatorial tradition. Here, an exploration of the semantic basis (conditioning) is also taken up. Obviously the nature of *samāsānta* suffixation is not semantic *per se;* but in its role in compound accentuation the *samāsānta* suffixation is irrevocably related semantically to accentuation of a compound. Thus a *samāsānta* is only a 'sense-less[1] morpheme but because the *samāsāntodātta* is governed by semantic conditions it becomes crucial in a semantic role in the accentuation of compounds. The morphological and phonological functions of the *samāsānta* suffix are obvious.

## 2.2 Types of *samāsānta*

Wackernagel (1905), who treated *samāsānta* in compound composition lists four types of *samāsānta, -ka, -i, -ya and -a.* He provides extensive attestation for each of these types, too. He talks of the elision of *samāsānta* and the substitution of *-i* by *-a.*

The *A* lists the following as *samāsānta* suffixes-(अ), -ac (अच्), *-ṭac* (टच्), *-ṣac* (षच्), -ap (अप), *-asic*(असिच्), *-anic* (अनिच्), *-ic* (इच्) *-kap* (कप्). These types can be broadly classified by their respective suffixation of *tp* and *bv* compounds (those dealing with suffixation in *dvigu* and *dvandva* are not dealt with here).

The need for a variety of suffixes for the same process of morphological closure (of compounds) is due to the differences in the final ending of the suffix, the *anubandha-s,*. This is more generally discussed in Chapter 2.7 wherein the examples are provided from Devasthali (1967) to highlight the dropping of the *anubandha* and its relation to the *samāsānta.*[6]

Most compounds take *samāsānta* suffix at the end of the final member but it is not a universal rule and is debarred from *samāsa* formation in special instances (A 5.4.69-72).

## 2.3 Encapsulation of *sūtra-s* Governing *samāsānta* Suffixation in *tp* and *bv* Compounds.

The type of *samāsānta* suffixes are classified following the *A* order. The primary function of the *samāsānta* suffix is to bring about the morphological closure of the compound concerned and to add the final IT to the compound. As to why there is such a variety of suffixes to bring about the same function is a moot point in addressing the details of *samāsānta* types or kinds.

Since the focus of this thesis is primarily on the accentuation of *bv* and *tp* and the related morphological process of *samāsānta* suffixation, only those *sūtra-s* addressing (specifically) *bv and tp* are dealt with in this classification. Although we are aware that *samāsānta* suffixation in its fullest implication can only be understood by dealing with every *sūtra* under *A* 5.4.68 in detail, in order to do justice to the breadth of the topic entailed, only those *sūtra-s* of the *5th adhyāya* 4th *pāda* are dealt with which have relevance to *bv* and *tp samāsānta* suffixation. Wherever a *samāsānta* suffix plays its role as a morphological trace vis -á -vis *bv* and *tp* formation, all those instances have been cited. Examples for the instances of suffixation are from the *Kāśikā (Kāś)*.

| *samāsānta* | Examples | *sūtra* no. | *sūtra* |
|---|---|---|---|
| pertaining to all compounds | | | |
| -अ | ललाटपुरम् | 5.4.74 | *ṛkpūrabdhūḥ* |
| | नान्दिपुरम् | | *pathāmā-nakṣe* |
| -अच् | प्रतिसामम् | 5.4.75 | *ac pratyanvavapūrvāts-* |
| | अनुसामम् | | *āmalomnaḥ* |
| | अवसामम् | | |
| | लवणाक्षम् | 5.4.76 | *akṣno adaraśanāt* |
| irregular formations | | | |

| | | | |
|---|---|---|---|
| | अचतुर | 5.4.77 | *acatura-vicatura* |
| | विचतुर | | *sucatura-strīpuṁsau* |
| | सुचतुर | | *dhenvanaḍuha-ṛksāma-vāṅmanasa-* |
| | the other examples are *dvandva* | | *akṣibhruva-dāragava-ūrvaṣṭhiva-padaṣṭhīva-naktamdiva-rātrindiva-ahārdiva-sarajasa-niśśreyasa-puruṣāyuṣa-dvyāyuṣa- tryāyuṣa- ṛgyajuṣa-jātokṣa-mahokṣa-vṛdhokṣa-upaśuna-goṣṭhaśvāḥ* |
| likely occurence of | | | |
| -अच् | ब्रह्मवर्च्चसम् | 5.4.78 | *brahmahastibhyām varccasaḥ* |
| | हस्तिवर्च्चसम् | | |
| | *vārttika* | | |
| | पल्लयवर्च्चसम् | | |
| | राजवर्च्चसम् | | |
| | अवतमसम् | 5.4.79 | *avasamandhebhyastamasaḥ* |
| | रान्तमसम् | | |
| | अन्धतमसम् | | |
| | श्व. श्रेयसम् | 5.4.80 | *śvaso vasīyahśreyasaḥ* |
| | अनुरहसम् | 5.4.81 | *anvavataptādrahasaḥ* |
| | अवरहसम् | | |
| | तप्तरहसम् | | |
| | प्रत्युरसम् | 5.4.82 | *prateruraśaḥ saptamīsthāt* |
| | अनुगवं यानं | 5.4.83 | *anugavam āyāme* |
| | द्विस्तावा वेदि: | 5.4.84 | *dvistāvā tristāvā vediḥ* |

| | | | |
|---|---|---|---|
| | त्रिस्तावा वेदि: | | |
| | प्राध्वो रथ: | 5.4.85 | *upasargād adhvanaḥ* |
| | प्राध्वं शकटम् | | |
| | निरध्वम् | | |
| | प्रत्यध्वम् | | |
| | द्वयङ्गुलम् | 5.4.86 | *tatpuruṣasyāṅguleḥ sankhyāvyaydeḥ* |
| | त्र्यङ्गुलम् | | |
| | अतिरात्र: | 5.4.87 | *ahassaravaikadeśa-sankhyāta puṇyācc rātreḥ* |
| -टच् | महागज | 5.4.91 | *rājāhssakhibyaṣṭac* |
| | मद्रराज: | | |
| | परमाह: | | |
| | उत्तमाह: | | |
| | राजसख: | | |
| | ब्राह्मणसख: | | |
| | परमगव: | 5.4.92 | *goratadhitaluki* |
| | उत्तमगव: | | |
| | पंचगवम् | | |
| | दशगवम् | | |
| | देवदत्तोर: | 5.4.93 | *agrākhyāyāmurasaḥ* |
| | उपानसम् | 5.4.94 | *anośmāyassarasām jātisamjṃayoḥ* |
| | अकृताश्म: | जाति: | |
| | मण्डूकसरसम् | | |
| | महानसम् | | |
| | पिण्डाश्म: | | |
| | लोहितायसम् | संज्ञा | |

| | | | |
|---|---|---|---|
| | जलसप्सम् | | |
| | ग्रामतक्षः | 5.4.95 | *grāmakauṭābhyām ca takṣ naḥ* |
| | कौटतक्षः | | |
| | अतिश्वो- वराहः | 5.4.96 | *ateḥ śunaḥ* |
| | आकर्षश्वः | 5.4.97 | *upāmanadaprāṇiṣu* |
| | फलकश्वः | | |
| | उत्तरसक्थम् | 5.4.98 | *uttaramṛgapurvācca sakth-naḥ* |
| | द्विनावम् | 5.4.99 | *nāvo dvigoḥ* |
| | त्रिनावम् | | |
| | अर्द्धनावम् | 5.4.100 | *ardhācca* |
| | अर्धखारम् | 5.4.101 | *khāryāḥ prācam* |
| | अर्धखारी | | |
| | द्वियञ्जलम् | 5.4.102 | *dvitribhyāmamjaleḥ* |
| | हस्तिचर्मम् | 5.4.103 | *anasantānnapuṁ-sakāc chandasi* |
| | जानपदः | 5.4.104 | *brahmaṇo jānapad-ākhyāyām* |
| | कुब्रह्मः (कुब्रह्मा) महाब्रह्मः (/महाब्रह्मा) | 5.4.105 | *kumahadbyām-anyatarasyām* |
| | | 5.4.106 5.4.112 | Are occurences of ṭac in *dvandva* and avyayībhāva |
| *samāsānta* in *bv* | | | |
| -डच् | उपदशाः उपविंशाः | 5.4.73 | *bahuvrihau sankhyeye ḍac abahugaṇāt* |
| -षच् | दीर्घसक्थः | 5.4.113 | *bahuvrīhau sakthyaksṇoḥ* |

| | | | |
|---|---|---|---|
| | कल्याणक्ष: | | *svāṅgātṣac* |
| | लोहिताक्ष: | | |
| | विशालाक्ष: | | |
| | द्वयंङुलंदारु | 5.4.114 | *aṅgruler dāruṇi* |
| | त्रयंङ्गलंदारु | | |
| | पंचांगुलं | | |
| | द्विमूर्ध: | 5.4.115 | *dvitribhyām sa mūrddhnaḥ* |
| | त्रिमूर्ध: | | |
| -अप् | कल्याणी- | 5.4.116 | *appūraṇi pramāṇyoḥ* |
| | पंचमा- | | |
| | रात्रय: | | |
| | अन्तर्लोम: | 5.4.117 | *antarbahirbhyām ca lomnaḥ* |
| | बहलोम: | | |
| -अच् | द्रुणस: | 5.4.118 | *aññdsikāyāh sahjñāyām-* |
| | वाद्ध्रीणस: | | *nasam cāsthulāt* |
| | प्रणरा: | 5.4.119 | *upasargacca* |
| | उन्नस: | | |
| | सुप्रात: | 5.4.120 | *suprātasuśvasudiva-* |
| | सुश्व: | | *śārikukṣacatura* |
| | सुदिव: | | *śraiṇīpadājapada-* |
| | शारिकुक्ष: | | *proṣṭhāpadāḥ* |
| | चतुरश्व: | | |
| | एणीपद: | | |
| | अजपद: | | |
| | प्रोष्ठपाद: | | |

| | | | |
|---|---|---|---|
| | अहल: | 5.4.121 | *nañduḥsubhyoḥ* |
| | (अहलि) | | *halisakthyor antarasyām* |
| | (दुर्हलि) | | |
| | असक्थ: | | |
| | (दुसक्थि:) | | |
| | सुसक्थ: | | |
| | (सुसक्थि:) | | |
| -असिच् | अप्रजा | 5.4.122 | *nityamasic* |
| | दुष्प्रजा | | *prajāmedhayoḥ* |
| | अमेधां | | |
| | दुर्मेधा | | |
| | सुमेधा | | |
| | बहुप्रजा | 5.4.123 | *bahuprajāścchandasi* |
| -अनिच् | कल्याणधर्मन् | 5.4.124 | *dharmādanic kevalāt* |
| | प्रियधर्मा | | |
| | सुजम्भा | 5.4.125 | *jambhā suharītatṛṇa* |
| | हरितजम्भा | | *somebhyaḥ* |
| | तृणजम्भा | | |
| | सोमजम्भा | | |
| | दक्षिणेर्मा मृग: | 5.4.126 | *daksinermā lubhdhayoge* |
| -इच् | केशाकेशी | 5.4.127 | ic *karmavyatiharē* |
| | द्विदण्डया | 5.4.128 | *dvidaṇḍyādibhyaś ca* |
| | दिभ्य: | | |
| -कप् | व्यूढोरस्क: | 5.4.151 | *uraḥ prabhṛtibhyaḥ kap* |
| | प्रियसर्पिष्क: | | |
| | अवमुक्तोपानस्क: | | |
| | बुदण्डिका | 5.4.152 | *inaḥ striyām* |
| | बहुछत्रिका: | | |

| | | |
|---|---|---|
| बहुस्वामिका | | |
| बहुकुमारीको | 5.4.153 | *nadyṛtaś ca* |
| देशः | | |
| बहुब्रह्मबन्धूकः | | |
| बहुकर्तृकः | | |
| बहुकट्वाकः | 5.4.154 | *śeṣād vibhāṣā* |
| बहुमालाकः | | |
| बहुमालः | | |
| बहुवीणकः | | |
| बहुवीणः | | |
| बहुवीणाकः | | |

Semantic preconditions that debar
-कप् sufixation in *bv*

| | | |
|---|---|---|
| विश्वदेवः | 5.4.155 | *na saṁjñāyām* |
| बहुश्रेयान् | 5.4.156 | *īyasaśca* |
| सुभ्राता | 5.4.157 | *vandite bhrātuḥ* |
| हतमाता | 5.4.158 | *rtaśchandasi* |
| बहुनाडिः | 5.4.159 | *nāḍītantrayoḥ svāṅge* |
| कायः | | |
| प्रवाणी | 5.4.160 | *nispravāṇiśca* |

(*Illustrations from the Kāśikā borrowed from S.C. Vasu's translation of the A.*)

### 2.4 *samāsāntāḥ* (A 5.4.68)

This section deals with the commentatorial tradition in the analysis and understanding of the above *sūtra.* Each text and the comment of the author is taken separately. It is interesting to note that while the *Bhāṣyakāra* Patañjali was more inclined to probe the functional aspects of *samāsānta* nature the later *Pāṇinīya-s* concentrated on giving more emphasis to morphological considerations. Hence the real function of *samāsānta* remains ambiguous from the literature and its semantic property only a tantalizing possibility.

### 2.4.1 The Comment of the *Mahābhāṣya*

The objector's first query is *"what for is this grasping or contribution to the final of the samāsa"*. Is it to be implicated wherever there is a final? The *Mbh* answers that the occurrence ग्रहण is conditional - .

प्रत्ययपरत्वेन अपि एतत् सिद्धम्

This indeed - its occurence behind a प्रत्यय -is its function.

Further there is the question - What purpose does this occurence (as final in a compound) accomplish ?

The answers to the questions of the *prima facie* views comes from Kātyāyana's *vārttika* on *samāsāntāḥ (A* 5.4.68):

*vārttika* 1

प्रयोजनम् अव्ययीभाव द्विगुद्वन्द्व तत्पुरुष बहुव्रीहि संज्ञाः।

i.e. The function of the *samāsānta* is in the formation of compounds as technical categories, as *avyayībhāva, dvigu, dvandva, tatpuruṣa* and *bahuvrīhi*. Patañjali offers the illustrations प्रतिराजम्, उपराजम् as those exemplifying *avyayībhāva*. The objector then poses the doubt if the function of *samāsānta* is in bringing about neuter gender, in *avyayībhāva* compounds :

नपुंसकलिङ्ता यथा स्यात्। (refer *Mbh).*

Patañjali points out that gender is learnt from societal norms:

लिङ्मशिष्यं लोकाश्रयत्वात् लिङ्स्य। (refer *Mbh).*

By *A* 2.4.83 the formation of *samjñā* is the function of *samāsānta*[8]

#### 2.4.1.1 *dvigu*

The same argument is projected by the *pūrvapakṣin* who

counters whether gender is ordained by *samāsānta* in a *dvigu* compound. Not so says Patañjali repeating the previous illustrations. The *Mbh* provides the examples पञ्चगवम्, दशगवम् as illustrations of *dvigu*. The fact that gender is not conveyed is shown in the formation of *dvigu* compounds such as द्विपुरी, त्रिपुरी The objection here is that "then does *samāsānta* bring about *akārānta*". Patañjali answers that this is not so for there arc *dvigu* compounds where *akārānta* is not noticed. Patañjali goes on to explain that the *akārānta* of *dvigu* takes ङीब् at the end. Hence forms such as त्रिधुरी, द्विधुरी result.

**2.4.1.2 *dvandva***

The function of *samāsānta* in forming a *dvandva* compound is encapsulated and highlighted by the *sūtra A* 5.2.128.[9]

**2.4.1.3 *tp***

The *prima facie* objector who wants to explore the possibility that *samāsānta* contributes to neuter gender, cites the *sūtra A* 5.2.128 as being of relevance to, his objection.

To exemplify his rationale he cites the illustration of अध 'धुरा Patañjali counters this by providing usages such as निर्धुरः in masculine and repeats the maxim that gender is learnt from societal norms.

The examples provided arc उच्चधुरः, नीचधुरः and Patañjali in addition comments that the *svara* of the *bv* is *pūrvapada-prakṛtisvara*.

**Summary**

Kātyāyana clearly defends the purpose of *samāsānta* as that of bringing about designation. Patañjali by providing the appropriate illustrations shows that gender is learnt from societal norms.

**2.4.2 The Comment from the *Kāśikā***

*Kāś* describes the nature of *samāsāntāḥ* (*A* 5.4.68) as an *adhikāra* rule whose force in application extends up to the end of the *taddhita prakaraṇam.* Describing the process of suffixation Kāś points out that the *samāsanta* occurs after the penultimate *pratyaya* of a compound.

> **आ पादपरिसमाप्तेः ये प्रत्यया विहितास्ते समासस्यान्त अवयवा-एकदेशा भवन्ति। तद् ग्रहणेन गृह्यन्त इति वेदितव्यम्।**

The conditions (प्रत्यय परत्व सामीप्य) for the process of suffixation is taken up by *Nyāsa* and *Padamañjarī* in their respective elaborations. नाव्ययीभावाद् (A 1.4.83) is a *vidhi sūtra* and by अनश्च *(A* 5.4.108) टच् is brought about.[10]

The commentary of Kāś goes onto provide illustrations of *dvigu, dvandva* and *tatpuruṣa.* compounds other than those given in the *Mbh.* Specifically regarding *tp, Kāś* gives विधुरं, प्रधुरः which get accent by तत्पुरुषे तुल्यार्थ....... (A 6.2.2). The examples उच्चधुरः, नीचधुरः get accent by बहुब्रीहौ प्रकृत्या पूर्वपदम् (A 6.2.1).

### 2.4.3 The Comment from the *Nyāsa* (on *Kāś)*

It is in *Nyāsa* that one finds the elaborated conditions, laid down for the *samāsanta* suffixation.[11]

> अन्तशब्दः अयं सामीप्यवचनोऽप्यसति, यदि तस्येह ग्रहणं स्यात् प्रत्यय परत्वेनैव डजादीनां सामीप्यस्य।
> सिद्धत्वादन्तशब्दः अनर्थकः स्यात् इति मत्वा आह' अवयवचनाऽयम् अन्तशब्दो गृह्यत इति दर्शयन्नाह।

Thus *Nyāsa* justifies the use of the word Kāś -अवयव in the समासस्यान्तावयवैकदेशा. It is to dispel the doubt that mere proximity of *samāsānta* to a *pratyaya* will bring about suffixation. Suffixation requires not just proximity to the compound, but also, that the last *pratyaya* be a part of the compound. Clinching the conditions necessary for and characteristic of *samāsānta* suffixation *Nyāsa* has the following to say.[12]

> **समासान्तान् कृत्वा पश्चात् तदन्तेन समासः क्रियते। एवश्च तैः सह समाससंज्ञा भवति इति उपपद्यते डजादीनां समासावयवत्वम्।**

### 2.4.4 The Comment from the *Padamañjarī* (on *Nyāsa)*

*Padamañjarī* expatiates a little on the topic of the process of suffixation. According to Haradatta it is established that a *samāsānta* is not necessarily affixed by proximity to the end of the compound. In making the conditions for suffixation clear, *Padamañjarī* says that only by using the term अवयव meaning a part of the compound (अन्तशब्द) can the process of affixation take place.[13]

समीपवचनस्तु न गृह्यते प्रत्ययपरत्वेनैव सिद्धित्वात्।
अवयववचनं चान्तशब्दम् आश्रयता समासार्थात्

उत्तरपदादकृत एव समासे समासान्ता भवन्ति इति उक्तं भवति। एवं हि ते समासस्यैकदेशा भवन्ति, यदि प्राग् एव तान्प्रत्ययान्कृत्वा तदन्तेन समासः क्रियते।

"समासार्थे हि उत्तरपदे कपि कृते पश्चात्समासेन भवितव्यम्।" (काशिका 7.4.14)

### 2.4.5 The Comment from the *Siddhāntakaumudī*

The treatment of samāsānta suffixes in this text is brief and not all the types of suffixes are treated in the section.

## 2.5 Exceptions to *samāsānta*

The following four *sūtra-s* govern the exceptions to *samāsānta* suffixation.

| | |
|---|---|
| *na pūjanāt* | (*A* 5.4.69) |
| *kimaḥ kṣepe* | (*A* 5.4.70) |
| *nañastatpuruṣāt* | (*A* 5.4.71) |
| *patho vibhāṣa* | (A 5.4.72) |

Under certain conditions *samāsānta* is debarred from operating on a compound. In A 5.4.69 the condition laid down for the exception of A 5.6.68 is the use of a certain *śabda* in the sense of *pūjana* (adjectival denoting quality). Kāś repeats the *vārttika* from *Mbh* but it is in *Padamañjarī* that an explanation is found.

As has already been stated *samāsānta* suffixation is not a universal rule. The exceptions are also clearly stated. The four following *sūtra-s* govern the exceptions of *samāsānta* suffixation.

न पूजनात् (A 5.4.69)

किमः क्षेपे (*A* 5.4.70)

नञस्तत्पुरुषात् (*A* 5.4.71)

पथो विभाषा (*A 5 A .12)*

According to *Padamañjarī* न पूजनात् (*A* 5.4.69) does not mean that a *samāsānta* is not found in the word conveying *pūjana* but rather its function is different; that its relation to the *prakṛti* is rendered superfluous, *pūjana* does not refer to the term, rather it connotes the suffix that qualifies in that particular sense. If *samāsānta* had been grasped, the form would have been सुराजम्, सुराज but since *A* 5.4.68 is obviated, the form is सुराजा[14] The exception to *A* 5.4.69 is सुसक्थः, अतिसक्थः which get षच् by बहुब्रीहौ सक्थ्यक्षणोः (A 5.4.113).

किमः क्षेपे (*A* 5.4.70) similarly debars the force of *A* 5.4.68 when *kim* precedes in a *samāsa.* नञ्स्तत्पुरुषात् (*A* 5.4.71) debars *samāsānta* suffixation when *nañ* occurs in *tp* before words such as *rājan* - hence the forms such as अराजा, असखा, पथो विभाषा (A 5.4.72) debars *samāsānta* suffixation in a *nañ - tp* [15] Similarly A 5.4.157 optionally debars *samāsānta* suffixation in instances where कप् is addressed in a *bv.*

In the following instances, -कप् is debarred from *bv* suffixation. Each anomaly represents a semantic cause for the absence of suffixation.

1. न संज्ञायाम् (A 5.4.155) The suffix -कप् does not come after a *bv* when a name is meant.
2. ईयसश्च (*A* 5.4.156) -कप् is debarred in *bv* when the compound ends in the affix ईयस्

3. वन्दिते भ्रातुः (A 5.4.157) -कप् does not come after a *bv* ending in the word भ्रातृ when it means praised.
4. ऋतश्छन्दसि (A 5.4.15.8) the affix -कप् does not come after a *bv* ending in short ऋ.
5. नाडीतन्त्र्योः स्वाङ्गे (A 5.4.159) here -कप् does not come about after the words नाडी, तन्त्री when they mean the organs of the body.
6. निष्प्रवाणिश्च (A 5.4.160) The word निष्प्रवाणि irregularly formed without adding -कप् through the last word in a नाडी word.

In the sixth *adhyāya* and second *pāda* of the A, while discussing the accentuations of *bv-s* in *A* 6.2.197 one can observe an exception to *samāsānta* suffixation in *samāsa* formation. Thus मूर्धन् retains its न् not allowing *samāsānta* suffixation. When *samāsānta* suffix is added then too the acute happens only to the final.

*Paribhāṣenduśekhara* as well attests to the exceptions of *samāsānta* suffixation.[16]

**2.6 Feminine Suffixes and *samāsānta* Suffixation in bv-s**

**2.6.1 बहुव्रीहौ सक्थ्यक्ष्णोः स्वाङ्गात्षच् (*A* 5.4.113)**

The new suffix -षच् is employed instead of -टच् for the sake of the accent.

e.g. चक्रसक्थी स्त्री, दीर्घसक्थी स्त्री

By. A 4.1.41 the feminine of words ending in an suffix having an indicatory *IT* is formed by ङीष् and not by ङीप् *(A* 4.1.15)[17] which has *anudātta*. The second term *'saktha'* has optionally *udātta* accent on the final in a *bv*. Thus the relation of ङीष् ensures *udātta* and removes anomalies in accentuation. S.C. Vasu explains that *'saktha'* is the *samāsānta* form of *'sakthi'* which is itself governed by *A* 5.4.113[18]. Hence the forom is गौरसक्थः However if the word ends in then it is necessarily oxytone चक्रसक्थ: as it is formed by -षच्. Thus -षच् is employed for the sake of the accent in a feminine form.

**2.6.2. ऊधसोऽनङ् (A 5.4.131)**

अनङ् is the substitute of the final ऊधस् in a *bv*.

कुण्डमिव ऊधोस्या: सा = कुण्डोध्नी, घटोध्नी.

The feminine is formed by adding ङीष् (A 4.1.25)[19] and these words are always used in this form for the feminine only; no substitution takes place in the masculine as महोधा: पर्जन्या:

ऊधस् + अन् = ऊधन् + ङीष्

ऊधस् + ई = ऊधी (अ elided by A 6.4.134) [20]

**2.6.3 The Invariable Suffixation of -ङीप्**

By the *sūtra* कुम्भपदीषु च (A 5.4.139) कुम्भपदी is formed by eliding the final अ and पाद and then substituting पद् for पात् before the feminine suffix ई (A 6.4.130).[21] This substitution takes place only before the feminine affix ङीप् and nowhere else.

e.g.s कुम्भपदी, शतपदी

**2.6.4 कप् and Feminine Gender in *bv***

(i) इन: स्त्रियाम् *(a* 5.4.152)

The कप् is added to a *bv* the last member of which ends in इन् when a feminine word is denoted.

e.g. बहुदण्डिका शाला

(ii) नद्यृतश्च (A 5 4.153)

-कप् is added to a *bv* when the last member is a feminine word ending in long ई orऊ defined as *nāḍī* words or which ends in short ऋ.

e.g. बहुकर्तृक:

The above were instances of the *samāsānta* suffixation in

*bv* when feminine suffixes follow *samāsānta*. *A* 5.4.159 deals with instances of कप् suffixation when feminine affixation is not involved.[22]

**e.g. बहुनाडीकः, बहुतन्त्रीका**

The word नाडी is a feminine word formed by ङीप् that comes after a word denoting class *(jāti)*. तन्त्री is formed by *unādī* affix ई *(Unādī.iii.158)*. In "बहुनाडी" *"bahunādī* the long ई is shortened as being an *upasarjana (A* 1.2.48).[23]

## 2.7 *samāsānta* Endings, *anubandha-s* and *samāsa-s*

*Samāsānta* suffixation is elaborately dealt with in the section 2.2 and 2.3 with respect to suffixation, the classification of *sūtra-s* dealing with the morphology and the respective illustrations. One sees at the outset that the occurrence of the compound ending is not uniform or consistently regular, although the primary function of bringing about a morphological closure is achieved. It is curious to note that certain compounds end in '-am', some as *'an'*. As stated in 2.1 a *samāsānta* first contributes to the final 'a' of the compound. Its secondary function is the contribution of accent through the dropping of the *anubandha* concerned, (if an ending is *'ñit'* the accent contributed is different from the accent brought about by the dropping of a *'pit'* ending.)

In terms of the accent contributed, derived or devolved in the compound (except in the case where the *prakṛtisvara* is retained) the function of *samāsānta* becomes crucial to the *antodātta* of a compound thus accounting for the inevitable variety of *samāsānta* suffixes. Perhaps this is the reason that Patañjali refers repeatedly to *samāsānta* as irrevocably related to accentuation in compounds. The internal evidence in the *A* is also revealing of the fact that the system of *samāsānta, anubandha* (although this is not mentioned as a technical term in the *A)* and accentuation is one of interrelated complexity.

The ramifications of *samāsānta* and *svara* are dealt with in this section where an attempt is made to provide examples of the variety of *samāsānta* existing for a particular type of accent. However with respect to the function of morphological closure it is valid to argue that *samāsānta* is a *"sense-less* affix". It would be unfair to vastly exaggerate the observation of Pāṇini on the nature of semantic preconditions governing certain types of *samāsānta* suffixation. Yet, the variety of suffixes available seems to suggest a variety of endings. In view of this it would be worthwhile to note that although the 'a' is the morpheme contributed by the *samāsānta* the results of suffixation even in terms of morphology are varied.

Thus with respect to the function of morphological closure it is valid to deduce that the variety of (types) of *samāsānta* is not as crucial as the necessity to exist in varied *anubandha*s (or *IT* characters) which can serve to contribute to the function of accentuation.

### 2.7.1 A List of *anubhandha-s* Dropped by Various *samāsānta* Types.

(Devasthali, 1967)

| | | |
|---|---|---|
| *aṅ* | *a* | 5.4.75 |
| *anaṅ* | *an* | 5.4.131 |
| *anic* | *an* | 5.4.124 |
| *ap* | *a* | 5.4.116 |
| *asic* | *as* | 5.4.122 |
| *ic* | *I* | 5.4.127 |
| *it* | *I* | 5.4.135 |
| *kap* | *ka* | 5.4.151 |
| *ṭac* | *a* | 5.4.91 |
| *ḍac* | *a* | 5.4.73 |
| *ṣo* | *a* | 5.4.115 |
| *sac* | *a* | 5.4.113 |

An observation of the table proves the irregularity of the endings contributed by *samāsānta*. Morphologically each *samāsānta* serves thc purpose of closure and bringing about technical designation. But, with respect to *svara,* the *anubandha-s* fulfill varied conditions although the *svara* is predominantly *antodātta*. It is particularly interesting to note the order in which *P* treats *samāsānta* types. He seems to hint at the more regular suffixation in *tp* and therefore this section precedes *bv* suffixation. The irregularity is further confounded in *bv* when feminine suffixes are ordained *(Bahuvrīhi-dvandvāhnika,* 1974). Thus we can rationalize the purpose of the variety of *samāsānta* in terms of the heterogenous nature of *anubandha-s* in their endings.

## REFERENCES

1. Böhtlingk, Otto 2000
   approximately translated as
   "which does not alter the meaning of "(....samāsa)"
2. Cardona, George, 1983.
3. Sharma, Dipti, 1982.
4. गोरतद्धितलुकि (A 5.4.92)

   The affix टच् comes after गो standing at the end of tp compound, when no elision of Taddhita affix has taken place in forming such compound. (Trans., S.C.Vasu,1997)
5. Cardona, George, 1983.
6. Devasthali, G.V. 1967.
7. Ibid.
8. नाव्ययीभावादतोऽमृत्वपञ्चम्या : (A 2.4.83 ).

   There is no luk-elision of the case affix after an avyayībhavā compound that ends in आ, आम् is the substitute of its case-affixes but not when it is the fifth case-affix. (Trans., S.C.Vasu,1997)
9. द्वन्द्वोपतापगर्ह्यात्प्राणिस्थादिनिः (A 5.2.128)

   The affix comes in the sense of matup after a dvanda compound, after the name of a disease and after anything denoting fault when the thing is found in a living being. (Trans., S.C.Vasu,1997)
10. अनश्च (A 5.4.108)

    The affix टच् after an avyayībhāva ending in अन् as the final of the compound. (Trans., S.C.Vasu,1997)

11. Nyāsa on Kāś on समासान्ताः (A 5.4.68)
12. Ibid.
13. Padamañjari on Kāś on समासान्ताः (A 5.4.68)
14. Ibid.
15. refer Chapter 7 for further ramifications of नञ् in tp.
16. Paribhāṣenduśekhara समासान्तविधिरनित्यः 85
17. टिड्ढाणञ्द्वयसज्दध्नञ्मात्रच्तयप् ठक्-ठञ्कञ्क्वरपः (A 4.1.15)

    The affix ङीप् is added in feminine after the nominal stems ending in short अ if the affix with which it ends has an indicatory ट, or if the affix be ढ, or अण्, or द्वयसच्, or दध्नच्, or मात्रच्, or तयप्, or ठक् or ठञ् or कञ् or क्वरप् Trans S.C. Vasu 1997.
18. refer Chapter 2.6.1.
19. बहुव्रीहेरूधसो ङीष् (A 4.1.25)

    The affix ङीष् is employed in the feminine after a *bv*, ending in the word udhas (an udder). (Trans., S.C.Vasu,1997)
20. अल्लोपोऽनः (A 6.4.134)

    Of a *Bha* stem ending in अन्, the अ is elided. (Trans., S.C.Vasu,1997)
21. पादः पत् (A 6.4.130)

    For पाद् is substituted पद् when the former is *Bha*. (Trans., S.C.Vasu,1997)
22. नाडीतन्त्रयोः स्वाङ्गे (A 5.4.159) cf.Chapter 2.5.5.
23. गोस्त्रियोरुपसर्जनस्य (A 1.2.48)

    A short vowel is the substitute of *prātipadika* which ends with the word गो a cow and of that which ends with what has as its termination a feminine affix; when regarded as upasarjana. (Trans., S.C.Vasu,1997)

*CHAPTER - 3*

# SAMĀSASVARA (COMMENTARIES)

## 3.0 The Scope of the Chapter

The scope of this chapter is limited to an examination of *P's* accentual rules determining *bv* and *tp* compounds alone. The criterion for choosing the above said compound types for perusal is not an arbitrary one. The Indian grammatical tradition together with the work of the vedic exegesists have held that the chief method of distinguishing between *tp* and *bv* compounds lies not just in their intrinsic dissolution into *vigrahavākya-s* (analytical sentence) but also in their extrinsic properties *viz.* the characteristic of accentuation.

## 3.1 Introduction to the Chapter

*P* probably codified his *A* based on the varied nature of usages in the vedic and the *bhāṣā*. These rules are not independent of one another in their domain of operation. For example, the section of *sūtra-s* on the unitary nature of accent of compounds cannot be read without recourse to the rules of accent of suffixes, *sāmāsānta-s,* as well as rules pertaining to semantic preconditions that determine *prakṛtisvara* or *antodātta*. None of these rules can be studied in isolation without working through the synthesis of all the rules of accentuation, which are scattered across the breadth of the *A;* it would be a futile exercise to treat accentuation as the only behaviour of a compound.

An examination of the traditional standpoint on the views of the distinction of *bv* and *tp* compound accentuation serves to emphasize the importance of addressing the same through Pāṇini's rules. The earliest ascription of importance to accent is seen in the *Mbh,* where the example of *indraśatru vardhasva* is discussed. Patañjali in his *Paśpaśāhnika* takes it up very elaborately when he discusses the function of accent using the example of the compound lexeme *"sthūlapruṣatīm"*. To quote

> ''याज्ञिकाः पठन्ति। स्थूलपृषतीमाग्निवारुणीमनड्वाहीमालभेतेति। तस्यां संदेहः स्थूला च असौ पृषती च स्थूलपृषती स्थूलानि पृषन्ति यस्याः सा स्थूलपृषतीति। तां नावैयाकरणः स्वरतोऽधयवस्यति। यदि पूर्वपदप्रकृतिस्वरत्वं ततो बहुव्रीहिः ( 6.2.1 ) अथान्तोदात्त्वं ततस्तत्पुरुषः ( 6.2.223 ) इति॥''

From here on starts the original explanation of Patañjali on *tp* and *bv* compounds. However, the problem itself is as old as the *RV* where the examination of the *Veda* into a poetic *Saṁhitā* form and the grammatical *pada- pāṭha* form came to be the earliest distinction made in the function of *bv* and *tp* compounds. Depending on the type of analysis with which one wished to view the *Veda* the variant functions of *tp* and *bv* were also expressed.

## 3.2 The Nature of Accentuation of Compounds

A compound can carry only a unitary accent whether it be on the *pūrvapada* or *uttarapada*. The set of rules that directly regulate compound accentuation can be listed as follows:

3.2.1 अनुदात्तं पदमेकवर्जम् (*A* 6.1.223)

3.2.2 समासस्य (*A* 6.1.158)

3.2.3 बहुब्रीहौ प्रकृत्या पूर्वपदम् (*A* 6.2.1)

3.2.4 तत्पुरुषे तुल्यार्थतृतीया-
सप्तम्युपमानाव्ययद्वितीयाकृत्याः (A 6.2.2)

Taken as a cluster these four main phonological dictums govern standard compound accentuation. The relations between these *sūtra-s* are also complex as *vidhi* and *apavāda.*

Here the word *pada* is read in the large scope of compound accentuation. Hence the unitary accent that accentuates a word can be extended to the domain of the accent of the compound. At the complex level is the over-riding fact that many different *pratyaya-s* compete to contribute to the unitary accent. Hence it becomes imperative to trace the accent of the *dhātu, pratyaya, samāsānta* to understand the devolution by which the compound pada carries a unitary accent. Before addressing these complex patterns, it will be relevant to examine the basic phonological processes by which a pada is said to carry a unitary accent - for this an elaborate assessment of the commentaries on the above four sūtras is taken up.

### 3.2.1 अनुदात्तं पदमेकवर्जम्

***anudāttam padam ekavarjam (A 6.1.158)***

It is important to understand the relevance of elaborating the importance of this *sūtra* when in fact the chief concern is about compound accentuation. The property of compound accentuation is not determined by *'a'* rule but by a *'a set of'* rules operating at different levels - some at the morphological and some at the semantic. However, the singular thrust of the group of *sūtra-s* that determine accentuation is reflected in the property of the compound which carries the unitary accent. This is so because a compound also is treated as a word, a *pada*. In this view compound words too are treated as *pada-s* and come under the domain of operation of *anudāttam padam ekavarjam.* (*A* 6.1.158). Accordingly *samāsa* also carries only a single accent (with very few exceptions of compounds). Thus it is a preliminary but essential step to refer, evaluate devolution by which the compound *pada* carries a unitary accent. Before addressing these complex patterns, it will be relevant to examine the basic phonological processes by which a *pada* is said to carry a unitary accent - for this an elaborate assessment of the commentaries on the above four sūtras is taken up.

### 3.2.1 अनुदात्तं पदमेकवर्जम्

***anudāttam padam ekavarjam* (A 6.1.158)**

It is important to understand the relevance of elaborating the importance of this *sūtra* when in fact the chief concern is about compound accentuation. The property of compound accentuation is not determined by *'a'* rule but by 'a set of' rules operating at different levels - some at the morphological and some at the semantic. However, the singular thrust of the group of *sūtras* that determine accentuation is reflected in the property of the compound which carries the unitary accent. This is so because a compound also is treated as a word, a *pada*. In this view compound words too are treated as *pada-s* and come under the domain of operation of *anudāttam padam ekavarjam. (A* 6.1.158). Accordingly *samāsa* also carries only a single accent (with very few exceptions of doubly accented compounds). Thus it is a preliminary but essential step to refer, evaluate *"uccaiḥ udāttaḥ"* is referred to implying that the *udātta* is with reference to the vowel and not the consonant of a *pada*.

Kaiyaṭa raises a valid point by debating if the word *pada* is generic or particular. As pointed out in the introduction, the term *pada* should cover a variety of finished words including what is of specific significance in this thesis i.e. *samāsa-s*. Kaiyaṭa gives the *pūrvapakṣin's* view. Further comments on the contribution of *acsvara* or *halsvara* are revelatory with respect to the difference between *anudātta* and *udātta;* the former can rest on either an *ac* or a *hal* but the latter is solely contributed as *acsvara*.

अनुदात्तशब्दं च लौकिकं मन्यते। लोका हि 'उदात्तं पदम्'-अनुदात्तं पदं इति व्यपदिशन्ति। अनुदात्तगुणयोगात्पदमनुदात्तम्। तत्राचामनुदात्त-गुणयोगे व्यञ्जनमपि तत्साहचर्यात् तद्धर्मं गृह्यत इति अज्झल्लसमुदायरूपं पदमनुदात्तगुणयोगात् 'अनुदात्तं' इति सामानाधिकरण्येन निर्देश उपपद्यते। 'एकवर्जम्' इत्यत्रैकशब्देन प्रत्यासत्या पदमेवोच्यते।

However Kaiyaṭa himself declares that his personal opinion is that in the term *paśunā yajeta* the term *paśu* becomes prominent with respect to the sacrifice. Hence the term *pada* refers to *vyakti* rather than *jāti*. Nāgeśa clarifies that the *"uccaiḥ udāttaḥ"* is referred to implying that the *udātta* is with reference to the vowel and not the consonant of a *pada*.

ननु सूत्रे 'पदम्' इत्युक्तेः 'पदानि' इति भाष्यम् उक्तम् आहजातौ इति।

With respect to the syllable that is excluded, Kaiyaṭa points out that it is the *ac* that is excluded by *kṛtrima nyāya*. By *ekavarjam* what is meant is that the *udātta* on an *ac* is excluded, all other syllables being unaccented. Kaiyaṭa's concluding remarks on this section is that it is that *svara* which is most powerful that is in force in the *pada*.

अचस्तु ग्रहणे यस्याचः स्वर बलवान् सः वर्ज्यत इत्यनियमाभावः।

The principle referred to here is that of *satiśiṣṭa* by which a *pada* takes the *svara* according to a new rule. This is detailed under the commentary *SSC (A* 6.1.158).[1] Also the formulation of A 6.1.158 follows *matublopa* गुणवचनेभ्यो मतुपो लुग्वक्तव्यः governs the elisions that transform अनुदात्तः एषां अस्ति to अनुदात्तपदम् by *matublopa (vārttika* on *A* 5.2.94)[2]

With respect to the condition of a unitary accent in a *pada,* Kaiyaṭa in his comments on the reiteration of the purpose as a verse (i.e. *yougapadyam...*) has the following to say...

This actually refers to the provision for doubly accented or words so that they are not made redundant by *A.* 6.1.158.

अनेन गतेः पूर्वस्य पदस्य प्रकृतिस्वरः विधीयते, तवैप्रत्ययान्तस्य चान्तोदात्तत्वम्। तत्र 'युगपत्' ग्रहणमन्तरेण विरोधाभावाद्यौगपद्ये सिद्धे युगपद्ग्रहणमन्यत्र यौगपद्या-भावस्य ज्ञापकम्।

The *Mbh* also adds or emends that the syllable carrying

the *svara* which is *udātta* can also bear a *svarita*. By *udāttagrahaṇam* is understood *svaritagrahaṇam*.

*vārttika* 1

Kātyāyana points out that it is not merely sufficient to say a *pada* carries only one *udātta* (or *svarita)* the rest being *anudātta*. He gives a converse analogy to the rule. If the rest of the syllables were not mentioned to be *anudātta* then the दोष would occur i.e. of many *udātta-s* occuring simultaneously. Such examples are seen in पठिष्यति and ह्याचार्या. The *purvapakṣ in's* question is why is there a contradiction of all syllables in a *pada* bearing *anudātta-s*. In a step by step illustration Patañjali says that if the *vipratiṣedha* (or conditions laid down, exemplified by Kātyāyana) were not stated the *pada* will not convey an *udātta*.

**अनुदात्तत्वमनेन क्रियते, अस्ति च सम्भवो यदुभयोः च उदात्तत्वं स्यात्, अन्येषां चानुदात्तत्वम् ।**

Kaiyaṭa's clarification makes the case obvious. He says that if the *sūtra* had been formulated as नोदात्तं पदमेकवर्जम् it is as good as saying that the rest of the syllables in a pāda (except for the excluded one) are *anudātta;* Patañjali says succinctly,

**न अनेन उदात्तत्वं प्रतिषिधयते,**

qualifiying his statement completely as a definitive response. In his concluding remarks on this *vārttika,* Kaiyaṭa says if उदात्तम् पदम् एकम् had instead been formulated the rule would have been explicit and this is the same as Patañjali's comment (न अनेन उदात्तत्वं प्रतिषिध्यते)

In the *sūtra* of the *Mbh* heading the *adhikāra* property of *A* 6.1.158 the question is asked whether this *sūtra* should be an *adhikāra* or *paribhāṣā sūtra*. Patañjali states that if this were not *paribhāṣā* the force of the *sūtra* should be repeated at every instance where a *svara* is borne by a *pada*.

**अधिकार प्रतियोगं तस्य अनिर्देशार्थ इति योग योग उपतिष्ठते।**

The argument is further confounded by pointing out that

it would not be possible to comprehend rules of the 4th *adhyāya* (समानोदरे शयित ओ च उदात्तः *A* 4.4.108) and 7th *adhyāya* (अस्थिदधिसक्थ्यक्ष्णानङुदात्तः *A* 7.1.75; if it were *adhikāra*. Thus there is अव्याप्ति here according to Kaiyaṭa if A 6.1.158 is treated as an *adhikāra*.

*vārttika* 2

This *vārttika* attempts at reformulating the *sūtra* under consideration in terms of the *udātta* which is excluded. While *A* 6.1.158 mentions accentuation of a word in terms of *anudātta* it actually reflects the presence of the unitary *udātta* on a *pada*. Kātyāyana by using the term *ananudātta* rephrases the *sūtra* in terms of the *udātta*. Patañjali clarifies the need for using the term *ananudātta* as follows:

**न उदात्तः-अनुदात्तः, न अनुदात्तः - अननुदात्तः। एकः अननुदात्तोऽस्मिंस्तदिदमेकाननुदात्तम् एकानानुदात्त्वात् इति**

Kaiyaṭa says that in fact this *paribhāṣā* can even be formulated as एकाननुदात्तं पदम्. By saying this he only seems to give and reflect the opinion of the objector. Nāgeśa goes further in saying that the *sūtra* can even be expressed as एकोदात्तं पदम्.

In the dialectic that ensues Patañjali explains that the purpose of phrasing the *sūtra* as done by *P* is specific. In referring to the accentuation (of the rest of the syllables) in terms of the *anudātta* the possibility of *udātta* or *svarita* accounting for the unitary accent is ensured. If as Nāgeśa comments (reflecting the views of the objector) that this *paribhāṣā sūtra* be represented as एकोदात्तं पदम्, then *svarita* would not be comprehended as a *svara*.

*vārttika* 3

**एकवर्जमिति चाप्रसिद्धिः सन्देहात्।**

What is excluded ? It is not certain if one of the syllables is actually excluded - the following *vārttika* is a discussion regarding the accent that is excluded in a *pada*. In response to this doubt comes forth the following answer.

*vārttika* 4

सिद्धं तु यस्मिन्ननुदात्त उदात्त्वचनानर्थक्यं तद्वर्जम्।

This *vārttika* makes explicit that *anudātta* does not refer to *udātta*. Thus in the formulation of the *sūtra* the one excluded *(udātta)* is made different or rendered apart from the rest of the syllables.

*vārttika* 5

प्रकृतिप्रत्यययोः स्वरस्य सावकाशत्वादप्रसिद्धिः।

The *udātta* can be essentially derived from the *pratyaya* or *prakṛti*. The purpose of bringing this up is to show the evolution of the unitary accent. Is it contributed by the *pratyaya* or is it the contribution of the *prakṛti* ? Patañjali provides illustrations for both instances too.

प्रकृतिस्वर : - पचति, पठति

प्रत्ययस्वर - समत्वम्, सिमत्वम्

उभयं - कृर्तव्यम्, कर्त्तव्यम्

The discussion following this *vārttika* is best encapsulated in the words of Nāgeśa.

परत्वस्य पूर्वविप्रतिषेधेन बाधात् कथं प्रकृतिस्वरस्य बाधाकत्वम् आह-धातुस्वर इति। प्रत्ययत्वप्रयुक्तस्वरस्य प्रत्यय सन्नियोग शिष्टत्वात् धातुत्वप्रयुक्तस्वरस्य सति शिष्टत्वम् इति भावः।

This question of whether accent is contributed by *dhātu* or *pratyaya* leads to the discussion of *satiśiṣṭasvara* later ( परनित्यान्तरङ्गापवादैः स्वरैर्व्यवस्था सतप्रकृतिशिष्टेन च ). In the words of G. Cardona the principle, by which *satiśiṣṭa* works, is encapsulated and discussed under the *vārttika* dealing with the force of *satiśiṣṭa svara* (cf 3.2.1.2.3).

Thus in Kaiyaṭa's words examples are provided for the mechanism by which *satiśiṣṭa* works.

सति शिष्टबलीयस्त्वाद्धि 'कर्तव्यम्' इत्यादौ प्रकृतिस्वरं बाधित्वा

प्रत्ययस्वरः भवति। गोपायतीत्यादौ धातुस्वरः एव सतिशिष्ट इति प्रत्ययस्वराभावः।

How does *satiśiṣṭa* operate in such a way that in some instances *pratyayasvara* is got and in others *prakṛtisvara* is obtained ? The self-explanatory and clarificatory *vārttika* 6 deals with this

*vārttika* 6

सिद्धं तु प्रकृतिस्वरबलीयस्त्वात्प्रत्ययस्वरभाव :।

By this vārttika accent ordained by *prakṛtisvara* takes precedence over *pratyaysvara* in a grammatical operation regarding accentuation, *vārttika* 7 which addresses the problem by making mention of the principle of *satiśiṣṭa.*

*vārttika* 7

सति शिष्टस्वरबलीयस्त्वम् च।

This *vārttika* emphasizes the fact that by the principle of *satiśiṣṭa,* a *sūtra,* a newly taught rule, takes precedence over one occuring before it. The ramifications of the relationship of *satiśiṣṭa* to the force of a *para sūtra* is more extensively discussed in *vārttika* 8.

*vārttika* 8

तत् च अनेकप्रत्ययसमासप्तार्थम्।

The resolution of the competition for contribution to the unitary accent rests finally on the principle of *satiśiṣṭa.* By this principle, accent ordained by a new rule cannot be revoked. Thus the accentuation becomes irrevocable. The purpose of *satiśiṣṭa* is exemplified by Patañjali as follows by using counter illustrations.

| | | |
|---|---|---|
| औपगव | - | अण् स्वर बाधते |
| औपगवत्वम् | - | त्वस्वरो-अण् स्वरं बाधते |
| औपगवत्वमकम् | - | त्वस्वरं कस्वरो बाधते |

In these illustrations, the accent of the pāda is double. It is to prevent the occurence of such exceptions that *satiśiṣṭa* operates according to Patañjali.

In terms of *samāsa,* Patañjali provides the following examples.

राजपुरुषः, राजपुरुषपुत्रः राजपुरुषपुत्रपुंसः

Thus *satiśiṣṭa* is the most forceful operator even when the सार्वधातुक accent (A 6.1.186) is taken into account.

The examples for such instances include लुनीतः where the accent of the *vikaraṇa* does not debar the accent of तस्

*vārttika* 9

स्यादिस्वराप्रसङ्गश्च तासेः परस्यानुदात्तवचनात्।

Here Kātyāyana concludes the discussion on *satiśiṣṭa* with the closing remarks that the *vikaraṇa svara* does not contradict *sārvadhātuka*. How the force of *satiśiṣṭa* operates is detailed under the following *vārttika* with specific reference to examples.

*vārttika* 10

शास्त्रविप्रतिशेधानियमाद्वा शब्दपरविप्रतिषेधास्सिद्धम् ।

If the definition of *satiśiṣṭa* given (cf. 3.2.1.2.3) is correct how do we account for the principle of *vipratiṣedhe param kāryam* (*A* 1.4.2.) whereby a later rule takes precedence over a prior one. This is the question that Kātyāyana raises and is best expressed in Kaiyaṭa's words.

*Satiśiṣṭa* enjoins the accent fixed by a new rule flouting the one previously in effect. In the *A,* in lieu of a conflict of grammatical operations the *para* rule is in force. The example which highlights the force of *satiśiṣṭa* is explained by Kaiyaṭa taking up the example from the *Mbh* - *gopāyati* The formation of accentuation in this word is taken up by later commentaries too such as *SSC.*

It was seen that starting from the section of *satiśiṣṭa* the discussion of the *Mbh* has been on the relative force of different principles of operation, the accents of suffixes and nominal stems, ending with a definitive statement on the nature, method and use of the principle of *satiśiṣṭa*.

As a logical and final extension of the theme the relative force of negative particles and *vibhakti* are examined in view of their contribution to accent.

*vārttika* 11.

विभक्तिस्वरात् नञ्स्वरः बलीयान्।

The self explanatory *vārttika* is an independent observation of Kātyāyana and is exemplified in illustrations provided by Patañjali.

अतिस्रः ................ अ + तिस्रः

तिस्रः has *udātta* due to *vibhakti* by the sūtra तिसृभ्यो जसः[3]

अतिस्रः (however by *tatpuruṣe tulyārtha...A* 6.2.2) has retained the *prakṛtisvara* which is the contribution of the negative particle (Kaiyaṭa). Nāgeśa sums up adequately.

As a summary of this section on the force of *satiśiṣṭa* are three concluding *vārttika-s* headed together in this thesis.

*vārttika* 12

विभक्तिनिमित्तस्वरात् च।

*vārttika* 13

यच्चोपपदं कृति नञ्।

*vārttika* 14

सहनिर्दिष्टस्य च।

The fact that the *svara* of the negative particle is more forceful than the *svara* of the *vibhakti* is elaborated in later chapters of this thesis where they .are dealt with in specific relation to the *samāsāntodātta* as well. The *nañ svara* also contradicts the *prakṛtisvara* brought about by गतिकारकोपपदात् कृत् (*A* 6.2.139). Even in the instances where *nañ* occurs along with the *dhātu* rather than separate from it, the *pratyayasvara* comes about. However,the most oprative or forceful *svara* is that of the particles, the *nipātana-s* as in अव्यथी.

### 3.2.1.2 The Comment of *Kāśikā*

The interpretations of Kāś are dealt with in the light of the explanatory comments of *Nyāsa* and *Padamañjarī*. An attempt has been made here to offer the explanatory notes of *Nyāsa* and *Padamañjarī* when the comment of Kāś is terse and cryptic. Rather than treating the explanatory comment of the original as a whole, here it is dealt with in specific reference to the cardinal comments of the *Kāś*. For example, the comments of *Nyāsa* on the rule *anudāttam padam ekavarjam* as a *paribhāṣ ā* rule is treated under a separate heading. The comment of exclusion - *ekavarjam* -is taken up for scrutiny under a separate heading.

#### 3.2.1.2.1 The *sūtra* as a *paribhāṣā* rule

To quote *Nyāsa*

**एकवर्जमिति । एकं वर्जयित्वेत्यर्थः। 'द्वितीयायाश्च' इति णमुल्प्रत्ययः। यद्ययमधिकारार्थः स्यात् ततः षाष्ठिक एव स्वरः संगृहीतः स्यात्। ये त्वन्ये स्वराः समानोदरे शयित ओ चोदात्तः 'अस्थिदधिसक्थ्यक्ष्णामनङुदात्तः' इत्येवमादयः सप्ताध्यायाम् ते न संगृहीता स्युः परिभाषायां त्वस्यां तेऽपि संगृहीता भवन्ति। सा हि एकदेशे स्थितापि सकलं शास्त्रम् अभिज्वलयति, यथा वेश्म प्रदीप इव इत्यालोच्याहपरिभाषेयम् इति। विध्यङ्गशेषभूता चेयम्। परिभाषा हि कार्यावाक्यानां शेषभावगता। यस्य पदावयवस्य स्वरित उदात्तो वा विधीयते तत्र शेषम् अनुदात्तं भवति।**

The discussion is about अनुदात्तं पदमेवर्जम् being treated as a *paribhāṣā* or *adhikāra* rule. If it is considered as an *adhikāra* rule then the force of the *sūtra* will apply only to the rules in the eight *pāda-s* of the sixth *adhyāya* and those rules such as **समानोदरे शायित ओ चोदात्तः अस्थिदधिसक्थ्यक्ष्णामनङुदात्तः** and from the fourth and seventh *adhyāya* respectively will cease to operate. However if the *sūtra* is considered as a *paribhāṣā* rule its powers of application are broader. As a *paribhāṣā* rule it determines the fact that where *udātta* or *svarita* are ordained in a *pada*, the rest of the syllables are unaccented - *anudātta*. Therefore *Nyāsa* comments that the rest of the *sūtra*-

s are *śeṣabhūta* - subordinate to this rule which is also *vidhi* in operation.

**3.2.1.2.2. The Accent on the Vowel**

Here the discussion begins with the query "What is excluded The debate is about the presence of अनुदात्त on the अच् (vowel related) syllable. The discussion in *Nyāsa* and *Padamañjarī* on this comment from the Kāś center around the nature and presence of the *svara* on the vowel.

*Nyāsa* raises a doubt if there will be a doṣa to *samānādhikaraṇa* when the *samjñā* rule *nīchaiḥ anudāttaḥ* (A 1.2.30) has described the quality of the *svara anudātta*. In response to the *ākṣepa* raised in the *Nyāsa, Nyāsa* itself counters that it is the vowels (अनुदात्ताच्कमनुदात्तं पदभिमहाभिमतम्) that are marked as *anudātta* in a pāda and by these the pāda comes to bear *anudāttasvara*. *Padamañjarī* offers a more elaborate explanation of this अनुदात्ताच्कम्

In a nutshell, to quote *Padamañjarī* -

**एकस्मिन् वर्तमाना अचोऽनुदात्ता भवन्ति एकमचं वर्जयित्वेति।**

When that is the case i.e. in a pāda the *anudātta* of a pāda is grasped then one of the vowels is "excluded" (it is *udātta* or *svarita).* To encapsulate in the words of *Padamañjarī,*

**एकमचं वर्जयित्वा परिशिष्टमनुदात्तमेव भवतीति विधिर्वा।**

In this context the *sūtra, anudāttam padam ekavarjam* operates as a *vidhi* rule. According to this *pakṣa* or opinion where *udātta* or *svarita* is ordained by *lakṣaṇā* (here, in the sense of description or definition) then by the absence of a regulation of the operaton of the *sūtra* as a *niyama* this matter (the *anudātta* being only on a vowel and not on a consonant) is treated separately or in disassociation.

When it is a *niyama* the pronounciation उच्चारणसंभवात् comes into being *(ucchāraṇasambhavāt)* due to the *svara*-s on the vowels. Later in the *Padamañjarī*, there is a rephrasing of the above explanation as follows :

On this too there are questions raised in *Padamañjarī*.

1. It is not known from the *sūtra* which (क:) is excluded or marked.
2. What is the nature of the rule in its force of application, as a *para* or *vidhi*.
3. Also *satiśiṣṭa* does not come into force here. Later *Padamañjarī* controverts this view.
4. If this rule is true *per se* how is it that in examples such as *'aupagavam'* there are two *udātta-s (dve pratyayādyudātta)*. For, as has already been mentioned in the introduction (scope of the chapter), there are certain *pada-s* or words or compounds that are double accented in character.
5. If *udātta* is ordained for only one syllable of the pāda which syllable is it ?

*Padamañjarī* concludes that it is difficult to establish if this *sūtra A* 6.1.158 is *vidhi* or *niyama* due to the problems discussed above. Perhaps with the usages available to the author of *Padamañjarī* the problems regarding the accentuation defined or determined by this *sūtra* became more apparent. Here, it will be appropriate to point out that *Nyāsa* provides examples that are not found in the *Kāś*. *Padamañjarī* gives more elaborate notes for the explanation of these. Keeping this in mind even the definition of *A* 6.1.158 as a *vidhi, niyama, para* or *nitya* seem controversial in line with the historical changes taking place in the language. What is most apparent is that the *sūtra* operates definitively as a *paribhāṣā*. The commentaries diverge on their opinions on its other powers of application.

**3.2.1.2.3 *dhātoḥ* (*A* 6.1.162)**

e.g. गो॒प॒पायति, धू॒पायति

By the *sūtra, dhātoḥ* (*A* 6.1.162), *udātta* is grasped at the end of a *pada*. Since the final vowel is marked by *udātta* the rest are *anudātta*.

धातोरन्त्यमचं वर्जयित्वा परिशिष्टमनुदात्तं भवति। *(Kāś)*

The examples provided are गोपायति धूपायति Here again we can observe the differences in the comparison of commentaries. *SK* gives the example as *(RV)*. Textual differences or changes could be plausible reasons for the difference in form through the ages.

*Nyāsa* provides the process by which this *anta-udātta* is got. By the maxims *"gupūrakṣaṇe*[4]*" "dhūpa santāpe*[5]*" "gupū-dhūpa" (A* 3.1.28) *pratyayānte* is obtained.

The designation of *dhātu (dhātusajṃā)* is derived through the *sūtra "sanādyantā dhātavah"*.[6] (A 3.1.32)

By this principle गोपयति धूपयति and get *antodātta.* are given. In these cases the accent is from the a *vikarana svara.* In the relative force of application between these *sūtra-s* is determined by the application of the *satiśiṣta* principle. To quote G. Cardona [7]

"Pāṇinīyas recognize that an accentuation newly taught supercedes one which was previously in effect (e.g., vt. 9 on A 6.1.158 [588]):

**सतिशिष्टस्वरबलीयस्त्वश्च**

................. referred to as the *satiśiṣṭasvara* (accent taught when there is a previous pitch on another vowel) principle it is sufficient to note that, although Pāṇini does not formulate this explicitly in the Aṣṭādhyāyī there can be no doubt he operates with the procedure in question."

The author proceeds to exemplify the operation in the example of *laviṣyáti* which would become *loṣyáti* instead, if this principle were not in effect.

**3.2.1.2.4 *Kāśikā***

The *svara* from an *āgama :*

e.g. चत्वारः and अनड्वाहः by

चतुरनडुहोरामुदात्तः (A 7.1.98)[8]

*Nyāsa* elaborates the process by which this accentuation of चत्वार is brought about. The *sūtra* in force is *cateruran* (*Unādī,* v.58) which brings about *ñitsvara.*

As counter examples to the function, of *dhātoḥ* two examples are provided to illustrate that the *svara* is *pratyayād-yudātta.* कर्त्तव्यम्-हर्त्तव्यम्

**3.2.1.2.5 Force of Application of *A* 6.1.158**

The principle of the operation of the *satiśiṣṭa svara* has already been dealt with. Here, the exemplification of the process is provided by Kāś with respect to *gopāyati,* the force of operation being only through the *satiśiṣta* principle. *para, nitya* become subordinate to the force of the *satiśiṣta* principle.

*Nyāsa* elaborates on गोपायति. By the *pratyaya svara* it is *ādyudātta.* Therefore in गोपायति the *svara* of आय is, stronger than the rest of the *pada-s.* The *pada* गोपायति gets *dhatusamjñā* by the principle of *satiśiṣṭa* through which there is prohibition *(bādhaka)* of *pratyayasvara.*

Even at this juncture in a detailed dialectic of the nature of the force of application of this *sūtra, Padamañjarī* remains critical of the absolute effect or force of the *satiśiṣṭa* principle.

**यदि सनिशिष्स्वर बाधकः विकरणस्वरः अपि लसार्वधातुकस्वरस्य बाधकः प्राप्लोति**

To bring forward the comments of *SSC,* Śrinivāsa Yajvan also comments or acknowledges the ordination of *svarita* in गोपाय नः.

To sum up, the unambiguous nature of this *sūtra* is in its force as a *paribhāṣā* rule. Though the earlier *Pāṇinīya-s* agree on the principle of *satiśiṣṭa* operating in such instances, the later commentators are either critical or accept its operation. The precise nature of the reasons as to why such differences in interpretation are present may be ascribed to the historical process of the commentatorial tradition and to the evolution of the exegetical process alongside the change of linguistic form in the available oral and textual traditions.

**3.2.1.3 Comment of *Svarasiddhāntacandrikā***

*Svarasiddhāntacandrikā* gives four illustrations from the *TS*

आस्यं चत्वारो वीरा जायन्ते।
दध्ना तनक्ति
गोपाय नः स्वस्तये
कर्तव्यं यजुः।

Here the devolution of the accent of चतेरुरन्

*(Unāḍī* v.58) is dealt with (by the *uṇādi* rule) the *'catu' śabda* gets *ñitsvara*. By the rule *caturanaḍuhorām udāttah* .[9] Thus in the word *catvāra,* the *āgama* gets *udātta*. By the rule *nabviṣayasya* the word gets udātta in *dadhnā*. The *prakṛtisvara* which dominates over the *ādyudātta* is brought about by the *sūtra*

*asthidadhisakthyakṣṇāmanaṅ-udāttah'* (*A* 7.1.75). *SSC* explains that in the examples already discussed in the *udātta* is got by *dhātoḥ.*

The other discussions in *SSC* center around *tp* and *bv* accentuation. At the conclusion, Śrīnivāsa Yajvan takes up a criticism of *Svaramañjarī* with respect to the illustrations provided in *Svaramañjarī:*

अप्रणिते स्वाहा। असतो वा एष संभूतः, असतः सद्यो ततक्षुः इत्यादौ प्राणते स्वाहा। शृण्वते स्वाहा।

Here in these cases by *śaturanumo nadyajādī (A* 6.1.173) one does not get *udātta* of the *vibhakti*. This, *Svaramaṃjarī* says, is due to the application of the *vārttika-*

विभक्तिस्वरान्नञ्स्वरो बलीयान्।

Śrinivasa Yajvan argues this point and asserts the process by which *'śaturanumaḥ'* one gets *vibhakti - udātta*. His point is that *Svaramaṃjarī* does not have to include the term when mentioning अन्तोदात्तात्–उत्तरपदात् to शतुरनुमः.

**3.2.2 समासस्य**

*samāsasya* (A 6.1.223)

**3.2.2.1 The Comment of the *Mahābhāṣya***

*vārttika*

**समासान्तोदात्तत्वे व्यञ्जनान्तेषु उपसंख्यानम् ।**

Patañjali provides the examples Kaiyaṭa clarifies that in the *sūtra* उच्चैः उदात्तः, अचः is got by *anuvṛtti* and by operation of अन्तोदात्त in a समास the compound gets the final acute on the vowel. How then is one to account for the accent on the last syllable when the compound ends in a consonantal ending? One of the points of accentuation in a compound is that *antodātta* is the characteristic of (W. By the *sūtra* (A 8.4.66) it is generally understood that *anudātta* becomes *svarita* when it follows an *udātta*. Both *svarita* and *udātta* are heard as the accents of the compound. As A 8.4.66 is *asiddha* to A 6.1.158 the *svarita* is not changed to *udātta*. This *vārttika* of Kātyāyana implies the relations between the *samāsāntodātta* and the consonantal ending of a compound. The question then arises why *svarita* is mentioned in the course of the argument and the answer is that it is to substantiate the accentuation of a *pada* as *dadhi* which carries a *svarita* on the final. This is an independent observation of Kātyāyana intended to supplement the view that as a general principle the accent is carried on the vowel.

Kaiyata elaborates the acceptance of the general principle that अच् by *anuvṛtti* is meant in the *sūtra*.

In the *Mbh,* Patañjali provides the examples of the consonantal endings that occur after the *sāmāsāntodātta* in a compound. As said above, the examples given are राजदृषत्, ब्राह्मणसमित्

In both cases the *udātta* falls on the vowel preceding the consonantal ending. However, central to the ensuing dialectic is the question - how does '*dadhi*' get *svarita* if *halsvara* is not ordained. The argument then goes back and forth, starting from the *prima facie* view that unlike an *ac,* a *hal* cannot contribute to the *samāsāntodātta* of a compound. The *paribhāṣ ā sūtra* is as follows :

**हल्स्वरप्राप्तौ वा व्यञ्जनमविद्यमानवत्,**

implying, that by the grasping of *halsvara* as a *samāsāntodātta,* the consonantal ending is non existent; for what is meant by *anuvṛtti* उच्चैः उदात्तः in is only that the अच् can take the accent. This is the view of Patañjali, who attempts to rationalize the *vārttika*. Again, the *prima facie* view is put forward that it is not the attainment of *halsvara* that is made impossible; rather it is the persistence of the consonantal ending in a *samāsa* that presents the problem. If this were to be true, Patañjali points out that in the case of *svarita* would not be taken as the final accent. Patañjali shows that by *A* 8.4.66, the word gets *svarita* - this being accepted as the general form of accentuation of a *pada* such as . However if the *paribhāṣā vārttika* is true, then *svarita* cannot be ordained in. With regard to the purpose of this *vārttika,* Nāgeśa opines that *paribhāṣā vārttika* may define the taking up of *halsvara,* (in his words

Kaiyaṭa however logically points out that the attainment of *halsvara* can be divorced from a consonantal ending in a compound. Consistent with his rationale he says that the absence of धकार in an intermediate stage for bringing about *halsvara* at the end of दधि points to this fact.

**To quote Kaiyaṭa**

**हल्स्वरप्राप्त्यभावाद्धकारस्य व्यवधायकत्वांत् ।**

The *pūrvapakṣin* had also objected to Kātyāyana's *vārttika* by saying that it is not the *halsvara* that is the problem in the placement of a consonantal ending of the *samāsa*. As examples he shows the case of द्विर्बद्ध, सुबद्ध.

Nāgeśa has the following to say :

**परिभाषायं हल्ग्रहणं व्यजनग्रहणं च इत्यर्थः।**

The *vārttika* that follows the discussion above is :

**प्रयोजनं लिदाद्युदात्तन्तोदात्तविधयः।**

Under this *vārttika* are provided a series of illustrations for the attainment of *ādyudātta* or *antodātta,* as the case may be. fold contributes to *ādyudātta* is added by *A* 4.1.105[10] and maxim the argument by showing that स्वरविधि is itself a compound which can be interperted as,

**स्वरेण विधिः**

**स्वरस्य विधिः**

**स्वरतो विधिः**

due to the principle of सर्वविभक्तथन्त. Further Patañjali A 6.1.116[11]) *svara* is taken even where it is not explicitly seen. This is to account for the accentuations of words such as मरुत्वात् and the plausible explanations for the accent of the तकार Patañjali says that in the *sūtra* उच्चैः उदात्तः when *udātta* is explicitly mentioned *svarita* is also included by *anuvṛtti.*

In the words of Kaiyaṭa :

**अज्झल्समुदायोऽनुदात्त उदात्तात्पर इति दधिशब्दे स्वरितः सिद्धः,**

thereby maintaining that when an *anudātta* follows *udātta* (as in दधि) it is *svarita* which contributes to the accentuation of the *pada.*

*Kāś* merely repeats the examples of chapter 3.2.2 dealing with the *Mbh* on *A* 6.1.223.The examples provided are

राजपुरुषः| ब्राह्मणकम्बलः| कन्यास्वनः| पटहशब्द| नदीघोषः| राजहणत्| ब्राह्मणसमित्|

*Kāś* emphasizes that this sū*tra* is an *apavāda* to obtaining multiple accents in a word.

### 3.2.2.2 The Comment of the *Svarasiddhāntacandrikā*

Due to the organization of the text, *SSC* deals with the final accentuation of a compound under two headings. The rule समासस्य is treated and commented on under the section headed *samāsasvara* and the *paribhāṣā-vārttika* of Kātyāyana as हल्स्वरप्राप्तौ व्यञ्जनम् अविद्यमानवत् under the heading परिभाषा प्रकरणम्

In essence, while *SSC* follows *Mbh,* Śrīnivāsa Yajvan provides further exemplification of the *paribhāṣā-vārttika.* In accordance to the manner in the *Mbh,* here, the commentary on the *sūtra* समासस्य is elaborated first, and later, the commentary on हल्स्वरप्राप्तौ व्यञ्जनम् अविद्यमानवत् although it is to be noted that in the text of the *SSC* the *paribhāṣāprakaraṇam* occurs before the *samāsa prakaraṇam.*

**3.2.2.2.1 *samāsasya A* 6.1.223**

*SSC* provides

e.g.s. वैश्वदेवाग्निमारुते and यद्यजमानभागम्

*SSC* says that this rule is an *apavāda* to the grasping of accent on multiple *pada-s.* Thus the implication is that the rule refers to the final acute which is the unitary accent of the compound. With regard to the illustrations where a *samāsa* has a consonantal ending *SSC* has the following to say -

स्वरविद्यौ व्यञ्जनस्य अविमानत्वात् हलन्ते इति समासे अन्त्यस्य अचस्य उदात्तत्वम्।

Thus, although the consonantal ending is allowed in a *samāsa,* the *samāsāntodātta* falls on the vowel preceding the final consonant. The illustration provided in *SSC* is

**3.2.2.2.2 *paribhāṣā - vārttika***

At the outset Śrīnivāsa yajvan provides examples of compounds, each an illustration of a compound ending in a vowel and a compound ending in a consonant. As in the *samāsaprakaraṇa* the example of a compound with *ajanta* is विश्वामित्रजमदग्नी and the example of a compound with *halanta* is अवभृथयजूँषि.. Śrīnivāsa Yajvan explains that the *samāsasvara* is not due to *halanta.*

अन्यथा यः अत्र समासान्ते स नोदात्तधर्मयोग्यः, यश्च योग्यो नासौ समासान्तः इति हलन्तेषु न समासस्वर स्यात्।

Reinforcing this is the statement:

**व्यञ्जनाविधमानवद्भवे तु हलन्तेषु अपि अजेव शास्तहहया अन्तः इति सिद्धमिष्म्**

With respect to the accentuation of the लिति already dealt with in the *Mbh, SSC* provides more illustrations प्रत्यय of instances, where a compound has *ādyudātta* as ordains or *antodātta* by धातोः In the previous instance जनतामेष्यम् has *pūrvodātta*. Other illustrations for the *sūtra* ञिनित्यादिर्नित्यम् (A 6.1.197) are औद्दालकिरकायत and तदिष्टीनाम्

To illustrate instances where the accent is on a vowel although the *samāsa* ends in a consonant Śrīnivāsa Yajvan provides the examples:

**सत्यकामिरुवाच and वृष्टिवैं वि श्वधायाः**

Śrīnivāsa Yajvan treats the *vārttika* स्वरविद्यौ अविद्यमानवत् with the example मरुत्वाँइन्द्रः He explains that this example gets its accent by the *sūtra* ह्रस्वनुड्भ्यां मतुप् Thus the *takāra* of मरुत् is rendered non-existent.

By the following lines Śrīnivāsa Yajvan shows that consonantal endings are always rendered non-existent. For in *dadhi śabda* the *dhakāra* gets *svarita* by the *sūtra* CA 8.4.66)

**दधि इत्यत्र धिशब्दस्य तादृशसमुदायस्य-उदात्तात् परत्वात्। नचैव सङ्घातस्य स्वरितप्रसङ्ग। 'आदेः परस्य इति घि'शब्देकारे तत्प्रवृत्तेः। 'हल्स्वरप्राप्तौ' इति धकारस्य अविद्यमानवत्त्वात्।**

Śrīnivāsa Yajvan concludes, by saying that there is no *doṣa* to the *paribhāṣā* rule, when *marutvāt* gets its accent due to *matup*. Quoting Haradatta he concludes:

**अनित्यत्वात् स्वरविधौ व्यजनम् अविद्यमान इत्यत्र न प्रवर्तते।**

It is due to its lack of force that *marutvāt* does not come under the influence of *svaravidhau,* a *paribhāṣā* rule. Instead the accentuation of a word as *marut* comes under the *paribhāṣ ā sūtra* हल्स्वरप्राप्तो व्यजनम् अवद्यिमानवत् and in the usage *dadhi,* by the same *paribhāṣā* rule, *dhakāra* as *halanta* is rendered non-existent.

### 3.2.2.3 The Comment from the *Siddhāntakaumudī*

The comment is cursory mentioning only the property of accentuation being *antodātta* in a compound. The illustration provided is यज्ञश्रियम्.

*Tattvabodhinī* explains that the illustration provided is *ṣaṣ ṭhītatpuruṣa* with the *udātta* being derived from the ईकार of श्री.

### 3.2.3 बहुव्रीहौ प्रकृत्या पूर्वपदम्

*bahuvrīhau prakṛtyā pūrvapadam (A* 6.2.1)

### 3.2.3.1 The Comment from the *Mahābhāṣya*

In the *prakṛtisvara adhikaraṇa* there is an extensive dialectic. The purpose of this *sūtra* is cited at the outset by Patañjali elaborating on the *sūtra* -

**समासान्तोदात्तत्वे प्राप्ते बहुव्रीहिस्वर अपवादं शास्ति ।**

In the words of Kaiyaṭa :

समासान्तस्योदात्तधिानात् बाधनार्थम् इदम् इत्यर्थः।

Kātyāyana provides the exceptions to the rule in the *vārttika* :

नञ्सुभ्यां नियमार्थं and not in other cases.

नञ्सुभ्यामेव बहुव्रहेः अन्तः उदात्तः भवति नान्यतः इति।

In order to understand the full import of this *vārttika* (an exception to *A* 6.2.1) it would be valuable to read the *sūtra* 'नञ्सुभ्याम्'' (A 6.2.172). By this *sūtra,* a *bahuvrīhi* formed by the negative particle नञ् or the particle सु, has acute on the last syllable of the compound.

Hence the examples यवो देशः, अव्रीहिः, अमाषः, सुयवः सुव्रीहिः (Kāś)

Kaiyaṭa sums up :

**''नानास्वरपदप्राप्तौ समासान्तोदात्तत्वविद्यानात् नियमेन तत् व्यावृत्तौ द्वयोः अपि पूर्वपदोत्तरपदयोः प्रकृतिस्वरप्रसङ्ग।''**

Kātyāyana covers yet another exception to *A* 6.2.1 under the *vārttika* 1.2.

*vārttika* 1.2

परस्य शिति शासनात्।

The sūtra in question is शितेर्नित्याबह्वच् (A 6.2.138) Kaiyaṭa offers the explanation that the *prakṛtisvara* of *pūrvapada* is retained due to the absence of the *uttarapada prakṛtisvara.*

The *sūtra* is शितेर्नित्याबह्वज् बहुव्रीहावभसत् (*A* 6.2.138). S.C. Vasu's translation offers the following explanation "After शिति, a word retains in a *bahuvrīhi* its original accent, when it is always of not more than two syllables, with the exception of असद्."

*Kāś* provides शितिपादः, शित्यंसः, शित्यौष्ठः

In true *Mbh* dialectic, Kātyāyana's *vārttika-s* amend the dictums of *P* where he finds usages to the contrary. Thus, though *P* has formulated the *sūtra-s* and it is Kātyāyana who clubs them together logically under A 6.2.1 as exceptions to the *pūrvapadaprakṛtisvara* of *bv*. Kātyāyana's next *vārttika* treats the logical course of citing the exceptions and the instances found thereof.

In order to understand the backdrop of this *vārttika* one must realize the conditions cited in the *sūtra-s A* 6.2.107 and *A* 6.2.108

उदराश्वेषु *A* 6.2.107

The first member in a *bv,* before the words and i|^[, gets acute on the final syllable, when the compound denotes a name. Examples of this final accentuation are from *Kāś* as follows -

वृकोदरः, दामोदरः

Thus this *sūtra* is an exception to *A* 6.2.1. *A* 6.2.108

A word before उदर, अश्व and इषु in a *bv* gets acute on the final, when reproach is meant.

*Kāś* gives

कुण्डोदरः, घटोदरः as examples.

Kātyāyana encapsulates in his next *vārttika*.

*vārttika* 1.3

क्षेपे विधिर्नमोऽसिद्धः।

Patañjali, refers to P's *sūtra-s A* 6.2.107 - 108 in offering an introduction to the substantiation of this *vārttika*. It is in Kaiyaṭa that we find an explanation for the full scope of this *vārttika*. According to him it is only because क्षेपे is a and rule that *samāsāntodātta* comes about in *bv*.

In Kaiyaṭa's words.

अनुदरः इत्यादौ पूर्वपदान्तोदात्त्वं 'क्षेपे' इति प्राप्तं

तद्बाधनार्थं 'नञ्सभ्याम्' इति स्यात् न तु

नियमार्थम्। विधिानियमसंभवे विधेः बलवत्त्वात्।

नञ्ग्रहणमुपलक्षणम् सोपि क्षेपिविषयत्वसंभवात्।

Thus Kaiyaṭa's opinion seems to be that in instances such as अनुदर the accentuation is a result of the relationship between A 6.2.108 and A 6.2.172 as a विधि or नियम rule, where the previous predominates in force.

In Nāgeśa's words we find a more accurate description of the meaning of the *vārttika*.

क्षेपे नञो विधिः संभवति इति

नियमोऽसिद्ध इति वार्त्तिकार्थः॥

ननु सुग्रहणं नियमार्थं भविष्यति इति आह।

Thus the विधि rule क्षेपे takes effect in final accentuation *sūtra* is obviated. What operates in accentuation then is the *vidhi* rule.

Patañjali adds to the exceptions (to *A* 6.2.1) by citing examples चाप्रियः and वाप्रियः which do not have *samāsāntodātta*. This statement is a prefatory statement to the following *vārttika* by Kātyāyana.

*vārttika* 1.4

अन्तश्च वा प्रिये सिद्धम्।

When प्रिय occurs at the end of a compound the अन्त (उदात्त) can optionally come about. Again it is only in the *Pradīpa* the full import of this *vārttika* can be understood.

**ननु च असत्यपि समासान्तोदात्तत्वे प्रियशब्दः प्रत्ययस्वरेणान्तोदात्त एव भविष्यति न च प्रत्ययस्वरस्य बाधकः पूर्वपद प्रकृति स्वरः।**

प्रिय शब्द gets *antodātta* by *pratyayasvara* and there is no contradiction from *pūrvapadaprakṛtisvara*.

Kaiyaṭa offers the counter example समपाद, where सम is सर्वानुदात्त and पाद शब्द is आद्युदात्तः

*vārttika* 2

Definition of the Term *prakṛti* in the *sūtra A* 6.2.1 Kātyāyana's definitive *vārttika* is प्रकृताद्विधेः

Patañjali points out that the term *prakṛti* with reference to *svara* is that of the *udātta*. However, such a strict adherence (o definition would leave insoluble problems in the accentuation of words कार्यप्रिय and हार्यप्रिय. Thus *prakṛti* refers to *svarita* as it docs to *udātta*.

अथवा स्वरितग्रहणमपि प्रकृतम् अनवर्तते *(Mbh)*.

Patañjali answers that it is by तित्स्वरितम् (A 6.1.185) which defines *svarita* "An affix having an indicatory त् is *svarita*" i.e. has circumflex accent. S.C.Vasu shows the formation of कार्यम्, हार्यम् with ण्यत् *(A* 3.1.124)[12] saying that this formation is an exception to *A* 3.1.3 which makes all affixes *ādyudātta*.

A definitive *vārttika* of Kātyāyana says that *A* 6.2.1 refers solely to *bv* compounds; hence the inclusion as the term *bv*. Patañjali substantially cites *A* 6.2.2. as semantic conditions for the accentuation of *tp* compounds. Referring to the appropriate and respective *sūtra-s,* he points out that those *sūtra-s* cover accentuation of and *dvandva* compounds which is beyond the scope of this thesis.

Thus this *sūtra* (*A* 6.2.1) refers solely to accentuation of *bv* compounds, an *apavāda* to *samāsāntodātta*.

*vārttika* 3

द्विपादिष्टेर्वितश्च पर्यायो न प्रकल्पते।

In order to understand this *vārttika,* Patañjali cites *sūtra* *A* 6.2.197

द्वित्रिभ्यां पाद्दन्मूर्द्धसु बहुव्रीहौ (*A* 6.2.197)

Hence, it is to be understood that *bv* doesn't get *samāsāntodātta* but that the accentuation got here is due to दिष्टिवितस्त्योश्च (A 6.2.31)

The section on *A* 6.2.1 in the *Mbh* ends with the reminder to the *prakṛtisvara* as *udātta* (Kātyāyana) *vārttika* -उदात्ते ज्ञापकं त्वेतत् and that *svarita* is grasped as well by the mention of the term *prakṛtyā*.

### 3.2.3.2 The Comment from the *Kāśikā*

*Kāś* clearly states that though *A* 6.1.223 ordains an *antodātta* this *sūtra A* 6.2.1 is an *apavāda* to *samāsāntodātta*. *Kāśikā* gives a list of examples with the marking of the origin of the *bv-svara*

*Kāś* provides the example cited in the *Mbh* समभाग which is सर्वानुदात्त (सम) and अन्तोदात्त as a counter example to the above cited instances.

For further elaboration of this *sūtra* the commentary of *Padamañjarī* is addressed in the main rather than *Nyāsa* which is an elaboration of the *Kāś* only to a minor detail.

### 3.2.3.2.1 The Comment from the *Padamañjarī*

Clearly defined in the words of Haradatta is the function of *A* 6.2.1. acting as an exception to *A* 6.1.223. Although *Mbh*, *Kāś* and *Nyāsa* relate the mode of accentuation defined by *A* 6.2.1 it is in Haradatta's words that the definition finds clarity.

तस्मात्समासस्य इति अस्य अनन्तरम् आरभ्यमाणः तस्य एव अयम् अपवादः।

He proceeds to provide a succint explanation of the term *prakṛtyā*-

यदि वा 'प्रकृत्या' इति अनेन स्वरविशेषे उपलक्षिते सत्ययम् अर्थः भवति-बहुव्रीहौ पूर्वपदस्य स्वाभाविकः यः स्वरः आद्युदात्तत्वदिकः सः भवति इति, एवं च यथा पूर्वपदस्यादि उदात्तः भवति इति उक्तेन समासस्य इति एतत् प्रवृत्ति उपेक्षा तादृग् एतत् इति युज्यते तत् अपवादता।

Clearly the 'natural' or original accent of the *pūrvapada* takes precedence in a *bv,* obviating the force of *A* 6.1.223, a blanket rule for accentuation in compounds.

Haradatta also goes on to explain the accentuation of नञ् compounds and exceptions to *A* 6.2.1 which were dealt with in elaborate detail under the section regarding the comment of the *Mbh.*

### 3.2.3.3. The Comment from the *Svarasiddhāntacandrikā*

The significant comment of *SSC* concerns the relation of the A 6.2.1 as an *apavāda* to *samāsāntodātta*. It clearly explains that the *pūrvapadaprakṛtisvara* is an *apavāda* to *samāsāntodātta* ol'*A* 6.1.223.

शतवंल्शं विरोह सहस्रवल्शा विवयं रुहेम

The ontological devolution of the accent is given as *antodātta*. सहस्र has मधयोदात by लघावन्ते द्वयोश्च He explains the counter example of समपदा as possessing सर्वानुदात by the force *of Phiṭ sūtra* त्वत्वसमसिमेत्यनुच्चानि.

Whether or not *svarita* or *udātta* comes about in this *bv,* only to be rendered non existent, and by the operation of the maxim the compound has *samāsāntodātta* which is contributed by पाद (आद्युदात्त)

The other example समभाग is not a counter example of the presence of the *udātta* and *svarita* in a compound. But succintly he says :

"असति अपि अत्र समासस्वरे भागशब्दस्य 'कर्षात्वतः' इति अन्तोदात्तत्वेन इष्टसिद्धेः।"

**3.2.3.4 The Comment from the *Siddhāntakaumudī***

*SK* affirms the सर्वानुदात्त nature of the word समपाद which is mentioned as an exception to *A* 6.2.1. *Tattvabodhinī* mentions that this exception is unique to समपाद and not applicable in cases such as प्रियवि श्व. The reason he mentions the latter, is to emphasize that it is only due to the force of the maxim 'सत्यपि सम्भवे बाधनं भवति the operation becomes complete in समपाद. However, in the case of प्रियविश्व such an application is not found. It is interesting to note that the compound forms प्रियविश्वः and विश्वप्रियः are both listed as illustrations of *A* 6.2.1 in *Svaraprakriyā* of Ramachandra Śesa.

**3.2.4. तत्पुरुषे तुल्यार्थतृतीया**

**सप्तम्युपमानाव्ययद्वितीयाकृत्याः**

*tatpuruṣe tulyārthatṛtīyāsaptam-*

*yupamānāvyayadvitīyākṛtyāh (A 6.2.2.)*

**3.2.4.1 The Comment from the *Mahābhāṣya A* 6.2.2**

*vārttika*

**तत्पुरुषे विभक्तिप्रकृतिस्वरत्वे कर्मधारये प्रतिषेधः।**

According to Kātyāyana, this *sūtra* resolves the anomaly of compounds to *A* 6.1.223. How ? The accent of the case affix of the *vibhakti* of the *tp* acts as a conditioning factor and the result is the *pūrvapadaprakṛtisvara*. In his next *vārttika 1 vārttika* 2.

**सिद्धं तु लक्षणप्रतिपदोक्तयोः प्रतिपदोक्तस्यैव ग्रहणात्।**

He confirms that the "conditioning" of accent is inevitable and effective.

Kaiyaṭa comments that this definition is only general

relating to the *svara* of *vibhakti* - विभक्ति विशेषम् अनुपादाय सामान्यलक्षणेन अयं समासः विहितः इत्यर्थः

Nāgeśa provides two different schools of thought on the interpretation of Kaiyaṭa's remark. One maintains that through the *sūtra* 'मयूरव्यसंकादयश्च[13], Kaiyaṭa's remark refers to the part concerning the presence of उपमान relation in a *tp*. Others however seem to consider the reference as being made to aspects other than उपमान-अन्यांशे. It is however unclear how the assumption of the first school can be made when Kaiyaṭa pointedly makes reference विभक्ति विशेष in his concise remark.

*vārttika* 3

**अव्यये नञ्कुनिपातानाम् ।**

Patañjali explains that the irregular formations of नञ् and कु and निपातन particles in a *avyayī* are formed as in

नञ् - अब्राह्मणः, अवृषलः

कु - कुब्राह्मणः, कुवृषलः

निपात - निष्कौशाम्बिः निर्वारणसिः

Where they are absent, as in examples स्नात्वाकालकः पीत्वास्थिरकः, which have accent on the final.

Kaiyaṭa offers the example of अकरणिं where the force of नञ्स्वर is greater than कृत्स्वर.

In Nāgeśa's words

**पुनः विधानस्य बाधकबाधनार्थत्वात् परमपि कृत्स्वरं बाधित्वा अयमेव स्वरः इत्यर्थः।**

*vārttika* 4

**क्त्वायां वा प्रतिषेधः।**

In Kaiyaṭa's words it is due to the restriction of words ending in past passive participles such as क्त that the अन्तोदात्त comes about and that is why it has to be explicitly mentioned to distinguish it from the conditioning factors mentioned in the *sūtra* under consideration.

*vārttika* 5

सिद्धान्तवार्त्तिकम् "निपातनात्सिद्ध"।

According to Patañjali, Kaiyaṭa and Nāgeśa the accent of the *tp* in the *sūtra* given are exceptions to the reading of *antodātta* in a *samāsa*.

### 3.2.4.2 The Comment from the *Kāśikā*

Here, the illustrations of each case and category implicated in the *sūtra* are given under the respective heading. The comment in *Kāś* is merely a repetition of those of *Mbh* but it will be profitable to examine the examples:

तुल्यार्थं - तुल्यंश्वेतः। तुल्यंलाहितः। तुल्यंमहान् सद्क्च्छंवेतः। सदृग्लौंहितः। सदृग्मंहान्।
सदृशंश्वेतः। सदृशंलोहितः सदृशंमहान्।

In each one of those illustrations, the force of *A* 2.1.68 (कृत्यतुल्याख्या अजात्या) operates and gives rise to the संज्ञा *viz. karmadhāraya* (formation by *[A* 6.1.20]). The *ādyudātta* is got which is preserved as *pūrvapadaprakṛtisvara* in *tp*. Where सदृक् contributes to accentuation in compound the *prakṛtisvara* is derived from कृदुत्तरपद by application of गतिकारक - उपपदात् कृत्।

तृतीया - *Kāś* does not deal with the relation of विभक्ति to समासानेदात्त but merely outlines the position of the accent, given the semantic constraint in the compound. शङ्कुल्या खण्डः - शङ्कुलाखिण्डः किरिणा काणः किरिकांणः

In the examples the accent is derived from कप्रत्ययान्तः In the latter किरि contributes to the *pūrvapadaprakṛtisvara* by the *Uṇādl sūtra* कृगृशृपृकुटिभिदिच्छदिभ्यश्च. (Uṇādi, iv.144)

सप्तमी

अक्षशौंण्ड, पानंशोण्डः

By सप्रत्ययान्त 'अक्ष' gets अन्तोदात्त and पान gets आद्युदात्त by लित्स्वर (ल्युडन्त).

उपमान

e.g. 1. शस्त्रीश्यामा (ङीष् is the प्रत्ययान्त that contribute to the Svara).

e.g. 2. कुमुदश्येनी (क प्रगत्ययान्त from कुमुद शब्द).

e.g. 3. हंसगद्गदा (स प्रत्ययानत from शब्द).

e.g. 4. न्यग्रोधपरिमण्डला gets purvaspadaprakṛtisvara b A7 3.5.

e.g. 5. दूर्वाकाण्डस्यामा In both these cases though the condition of उपमान is present, as it is षष्ठी tp and the accestuation is on the उत्तपरद अव्यय.

The Example providelare अब्राह्मण:| अवृषल:|

In all these is found ādyudātta.

The comments of Nyāsā and Padamañjanī are perfunctory and a this loading and merely supplement the illustrations of kaś.

The comments of *Nyāsa* and *Padamañjarī* are perfunctory under this heading and merely supplement the illustrations of *Kāś*.

**3.2.4.3. The Comment from the Svarasiddhānta - *candrikā***

Śrīnivāsa Yajvan using the example of सारागवस्रैजरदक्ष: explains the relations that contribute to accent at the out-set, in the section that deals with सप्तमीपर्वपदप्रकृति स्वर But in an example, such as देवकृतुमेनोऽयाड्वमर्त्यैर्मर्त्यकृतम् there is बाधक (contradiction) to the सप्तमी प्रकृति-स्वर by the power of the कृत् स्वर, if we consider देवकृतम् as *bv* (देवेषु कृतं करणं यस्य refer, review of literature).

In an example such as देवकृतस्यैनस: where the instrumental

operates (देवादिभिः अस्मद्विषयेः यत् कृतम् एनः फलं दुःखम्) one still gets *pūrvapadaprakṛtisvara* due to *sūtra* तृतीया कर्मणि।

Some illustrations from the *TS* provided to highlight *prakṛtisvara* are

कुर्कन्धुरोहितः, शुकबभ्रुः

Similarly, to provide illustrations from *TS* for the presence of *prakṛtisvara* in अव्यय, the examples in *Mbh* are repeated here, attested as

अब्राह्मणश्च प्रश्नोमेयाताम्।

With respect to the discussion between the relative force of नञ्स्वर and समासान्तोदात्त, Śrīnivāsa Yajvan has the following to say-

that नञ्स्वर is contradited in अपथात् पन्थामपिनयति only due to the principle of सतिशिष्ठ He does put to rest the retention of predittivara in द्वितीया by showing that it is अहीने द्वितीया, that the accent comes about but is तृतीसर tp it is due to the form of A 6.2.2. The Purvapada prakṛtisvara is got. In contradiction example उत्तरवेद्या, उत्तरवेद्याम्, the samāsa is due to विशेषण विशेष्य relation and not due to तृतीया tp savara.

The purpose of Śrīnivāsa Yajvan lies in explaining usages of the *TS* and in a critique of *Svaramañjarī* (which text has not been dealt with in this thesis). The plausible explanations for unitary accent of *tp-s* in the conditions of *A* 6.2.2 are explained and he points out cases where the illustrations seem to bring into focus and highlight the presence of *prakṛtisvara* in *A* 6.2.2.

Summing up, some of the observations of Chapter 3 are repeated in the final. The relations between these four cardinal *sūtra-s* are seen to be principal in influencing the acccentuation of samāsasvara. Some of the interesting observations on the relations of these four *sūtra-s* are:

(1) The force of the *sūtra* in a grammatical operation concerning accentuation ( *samāsasvara* ) is the *satiśiṣ ṭa* principle. To repeat the maxim:

**परनित्यानतरङ्गापवादभावैर्व्यवस्थितेः ।**
**सतिषिष्टत्वेन चेदं सर्वेभ्यः प्रबलं मतम् ॥**

(2) The exertion of the influence of conditions in each *sūtra* is also peculiar. Considering the examples provided in the SSC,

**यत्पदिबद्धा, ग्रीवबद्धमैनम्,**

the kṛt accentuation here is got by the *para* principle whereby गतिकारकोपपदात् कृत् exerts accentuation rather than तत्पुरुषे तुल्यार्थ which could have brought about accentuation by सप्तमीपूर्वपदप्रकृतिस्वर... Thus we see that in some cases the *para* principle also operates.

(3) However, the reminder by Kātyāyana of the power of *satiśiṣṭa* is to bring about bv-accent in examples such as कार्ष्णोत्तरसङ्ग which was discussed under that heading.

(4) The relations of *nañ* , *vibhakti,* and kṛt are best encapsu-lated in the *vārttika:*

**विभक्तिस्वरान्नञ्स्वरो बलीयानिति वक्तव्यम्।**
**विभक्तिनिमित्तस्वराच्च । यच्चोपपदं कृति नञ् तस्य**
**स्वरो बलीयानिति वक्तव्यम्। सहनिर्दिष्टस्य च इति।**

Śrīnivāsa Yajvan to illustrate this *vārttika* sums up in a 'step by step' elucidation.

In अचत्वारः, अनडुवाहः the accentuation of *vibhakti* is again contradicted. Similarly in अकरणि, the नञ् takes precedence over कृत् though the later by should have come into force.

In अतिस्रः vibhaktyudātta is not obtained due to the force of नञ्. It is due to नञ् that the accentuation come about by the force of तत्पुरुष तुल्यार्थ

In अव्यथी the *nipātana* contributes to the accent.

This illustration is provided by Śrīnivāsa Yajvan to elaborate on the ramifications of the power of *satiśiṣṭa* and other rules in bringing about the unitary accent of the com-pound. Thus, he highlights the complexity of this *satiśiṣṭ a* principle by which the power and order of many rules across the breadth of the *A* has to be taken into account.

As seen in the following chapters the accentuation of a compound is not simplistically ordained but many different factors of morphology and principles of phonology, as well, go to contribute to the accentuation which is diverse, althogh a certain pattern can be inferred from P's *magnum opus* the *A*.

## REFERENCES

1. cf. Chapter 3.2.1.2
2. कुम्भपदीषुच (A 5.4.139)

   The words kumbhapadi & C have been formed by the similar elision of the पाद: (Trans., S.C.Vasu,1997)
3. तिसृभ्यो जस: (A 6.1.66)

   The nominative plural (जस्) of (तिसृ) has acute accent on the last syllable. (Trans., S.C.Vasu,1997)
4. Nyāsa on Kāś on A 6.1.158.
5. Ibid.
6. सनाद्यन्ता धातव: (A 3.1.32)

   All the words ending with the affixes सन् and others are called dhātu. (Trans., S.C.Vasu, 1997)
7. Cardona, George. 1997
8. चतुरनडुहोरामुदात्त: (A 7.1.98)

   चतुर and अनुडुह् get the acutely accented augment (आम्) after the ऊ in the strong cases. (Trans., S.C.Vasu, 1997)
9. Ibid.
10. गर्गादिभ्यो यञ् (A 4.1.105)

    The affix यञ् comes in the sense of Gotra descendant after the words Garga. (Trans., S.C.Vasu,1997)
11. ह्रस्वनुड्भ्यां मतुप् (A 6.1.176)

    The otherwise unaccented मत् (वत्) takes the acute accent when an oxytoned stem ends in a light vowel or the affix has before it the augment न् (Trans., S.C.Vasu,1997)

12. ऋहलोर्ण्यत् (A 3.1.124)

    The affix ण्यत् comes after a verb that ends in ऋ (long or short) or in a consonant.

13. मयूरव्यंसकादयश्च (A 2.1.72)

    The words like मयूर and व्यंसक are treated as tp Compounds and irregularly formed tp compounds. The force of च is that of restriction.

## CHAPTER 4

# PRAKṚTISVARA AND SAMĀSĀNTODĀTTA

*P* merely defines the position of the *samāsasvara* in *A* 6.1.223. The nature of *samāsāntodātta* is elaborated in the main by Patañjali with respect to *apavāda-s* to *A* 6.1.223. The relations being to nañ , semantic motivations or morphological elements *(kṛt, vibhakti, gati)* dealt with later in this thesis. It is due to the influence of the semantic or morphological factors that the original *svara* or the *pūrvapadaprakṛtisvara* is retained. This relationship of *A* 6.1.223 to *A* 6.2.1 and *A* 6.2.2 was discussed in Chapter 3 in the backdrop of the commentatorial expositions.

In this chapter a tabulation of the exceptions to *samā-sāntodātta* and the instances of *antodātta* are given to distinguish between the illustrations of the two types of compounds dealt with - the *bv* and *tp*.

*P* clearly understood the diversity of the nature of accentuation and the difficulties that could arise there from. That is why he probably laid down the dictum in *A* 6.2.198 at the end परादिश्छन्दसि बहुलम् *(A* 6.2.199). It is essential to understand even the intricate subtleties underlying the distinction in accentuation (of compounds) prior to A 6.2.199. Despite the variety of the degrees of accentuation seen in the *Chandas, P* in dealing with *tp* and *bv* in *A* 6.2 provides for clearly defined types or kinds. These he formulates in *sūtra-s* that act as अधिकार either in the beginning or the middle of the pāda of the *adhyāya,* here 6.2. The principal *sūtra-s* defining accentuation in compounds were examined in Chapter 3. Particularly, the idealized situation accepted by the commentatorial tradition was explored. The nature of *antodātta (A* 6.1.223) and *prakṛti-*

*svara (A* 6.2.1 and *A* 6.2.2 and others) were discussed with respect to the relationship of the *sūtra-s* and their force of application in the *A*.

In this chapter a further complexity to the nature of accentuation of *antodātta* and *prakṛtisvara* as delineated by *P* is examined. The device and the technical terms that the author uses to describe these modes of accent are also listed. The terms used by him and *adhikāra sūtra-s* meant to be taken as *anuvṛtti* are :

1. *antodātta,* the *samāsāntodātta* -

   the final syllable of the final member of the compound carrying the *samāsa.* It is defined by *samāsasya (A* 6.1.223).

2. *pūrvapadaprakṛtisvara* -

   the "original accent" preserved in the initial member of the compound. It is defined as *apavāda to A* 6.1.223 as in *bahuvrīhau prakṛtyā pūrvapadam. (A* 6.2.1)

3. *ādyudātta* of the *pūrvapada* -

   *udātta* is ordained by *ādiḥ udāttah (A* 6.2.64) whereby "the first syllable has the acute of the *pūrvapada"* upto *A* 6.2.91.

4. *antodātta* of the *pūrvapada* -

   defined by *antaḥ (A* 6.2.92), whereby the " last syllable in a word of the first member has the acute". This *antodātta* is an *adhikāra* extending its scope upto *A* 6.2.110. This is seen in both *tp* and *bv*.

5. *antodātta-* of the *uttarapada* -

   whereby the "last member takes acute on the final (syllable)." It is seen defined with a condition-ing clause as in *uttarapadavṛddhau sarvam ca (A* 6.2.105)

6. *ādyudātta* of *uttarapada* -

   whereby the first syllable of the second member has

the acute. This is an *adhikāra* and is defined by *uttarapadādiḥ (A* 6.2.111). It is seen in both *tp* and *bv*.

7. *prakṛtisvara* of the *uttarapada* -

   by which the *prakṛtisvara* of the second member (*tp* or *bv)* is retained.

8. *antodātta* of the *uttarapada*

   which is the final acute of the final syllable of the final member of the compound. It is repeated as the *adhikāra* in *antaḥ (A* 6.2.143)

**Observations**

The accentuation as already mentioned is influenced by both the semantics as well as morphology. These could be obvious as in the instances where *prakṛtisvara* is retained by semantic motivations *(sūtra-s* such as *A* 6.2.2, *A* 6.2.3, *A 6.2* 4 etc.).[1] Similar semantic motivation can also bring about a polar effect, in essence contributing to *antodātta* as in *A* 6.2.195 among others.[2]

A *tp* may also preserve *prakṛtisvara* in the *uttarapada* due to morphological *(A* 6.2.139)[3] or due to semantic motivation *(A* 6.2.137).[4] Further, negation can act as a semantic influence and as a morphological derivative in bringing about the accent of a nañ *-tp* or a nañ *-bv*. These instances of *nañ - samāsa-s* are highlighted in the Chapter 7. (As a sequence the accent is a *antodātta)*. An *upasarga* influences accent in such an instance as *A* 6.2.193 bringing about *samāsāntodātta* (प्रत्यंशु: has *samāsāntodātta* as प्रति precedes अंशु the condition observed by P).[5]

In the light of this distinction in the position of the *svara*, a further degree of complexity can be addressed. The motivating factors for bringing about *prakṛtisvara, antodātta (pūrvapada* or *uttarapada)* or *samāsāntodātta* are :

(1) Semantic such as विभक्ति

(2) Semantic such as the motivations addressed by the term's meaning e.g. शरद्, वर्ण....

(3) Semantic and morphological such as negative particles as नञ् (observations in Chapter 7).

(4) Morphological elements such as कृत्, क्त, उपसर्ग, गति (observations in Chapter 5 and 6).

(5) Morphophonemic such as the syllables of the second *pada* following the *pūrvapada*.[6]

None of the above has an isolated influence on the accentuation. Together, the semantic and morphological factors combine to produce "desired" accentuation. The following table enlists the *sūtra-s* in their categories of the nature of accentuation.

| **Nature-Description** | **Sūtra Number** |
|---|---|
| 1. *samāsa-udātta* | **A 6.1.223** |
| 2. *pūrvapadaprakṛtisvara* | bv: A 6.2.1<br>tp:<br>*A* 6.2.2 - A 6.2.24<br>*tp: A* 6.2.40 - A 6.2.41<br>A 6.2.42, A 6.2.60 - 63 |
| 3. *ādyudātta* of the *pūrvapada* | *tp:*<br>*A* 6.2.64 - A 6.2.91 |
| 4. *a) antodātta* of the *purvapada* | A 6.2.92 - *A* 6.2.110 |
| 4. *b) antodātta* of the *uttarapada* | (Condition by the *vṛddhi* of the first syllable of the second term by A 7.3.12 &13) |
| 5. *antodātta* of the *uttarapada* | A 6.2.105<br>(A conditioning |

| | |
|---|---|
| final syllable of the last member. | clause (*uttarapada vṛddhau sarvam ca*)) |
| 6. *ādyudātta* of *uttarapada* | *bv* :<br>A4 6.2.111 - A 6.2.136<br>*tp* :<br>A 6.2.124,<br>A 6.2.126- 132<br>tp : Semantically influenced<br>A 6.2.133<br>*tp* :<br>A 6.2.134 - 136<br>*bv* :<br>A 6.2.138 |
| 7. *prakṛtisvara* of the *uttarapada* . | *tp:*<br>*A* 6.2.137, 139, 140<br>*bv* :<br>A 6.2.162 - 192<br>A 6.2.197 |
| 8. *antodātta* of the *uttarapada* | tp:<br>A 6.2.143 - 154,<br>*tp* :<br>A 6.2.193 - 196<br>*nan- samāsa* :<br>A 6.2.155 - 166 |

## REFERENCES

1. In sūtra-s such as A 6.2.2, 6.2.3 and 6.2.4 P mentions the nature of semantic conditioning on compound word formation in terms of accentuation. To illustrate such provisions, the following sūtra-s are provided. e.g.s

(i) तत्पुरुषे तुल्यार्थ (A 6.2.2)

Where the case affix, kṛt suffix or the sense of comparison, or an indefinite article affects the prakṛtisvara. (Trans., S.C.Vasu,1997)

(ii) वर्णो वर्णेष्वनेते (A 6.2.3)

Here when the term varṇa denoting colour is compounded with another colour denoting word, prakṛtisvara is retained. (Trans., S.C.Vasu,1997)

(iii) गाधलवणयो: प्रमाणे (A 6.2.4)

When the second term is gādha or lavaṇa and the compound expresses the meaning mass or masculine the prakṛtisvara is retained. (Trans., S.C.Vasu,1997)

. Thus prakṛtisvara is retained when semantic conditionings of certain terms influence meaning. The table in chapter 4 includes such conditions.

2. सोरवक्षेपणे (A 6.2.195)

By this sūtra the second member after सु has antodātta in a tp, when reproach is meant, although usually connotes praise. (Trans., S.C.Vasu,1997)

3. गतिकारकोपपदात्कृत् (A 6.2.139)

For an extended review, refer Chapter 5.

4. प्रकृत्या भगालभ् (A 6.2.137)

When the term भगाल occurs at the end of a compound, it preserves the prakṛtisvara. (Trans., S.C.Vasu, 1997)

5. प्रतेरंश्वादयस्तत्पुरुषे (A 6.2.193)

When the words अंशु and others have acute on the final when preceded by प्रति (Trims., S.C.Vasu,1997)

6. In the following three sūtra-s. an observation is made by P that the antodātta falls on a particular or certain syllable of the compound.

(i) क्रत्वादयश्य (A 6.2.118)

After सु in a bv, the acute falls on the first syllable क्रतु & others. (Trans., S.C.Vasu,1997)

(ii) आद्युदात्तम् द्वयाच्छन्दसि (A 6.2.119)

In the chandas (the vedic) a bv of 2 syllable has acute on the first syllable when preceded by सु (Trans., S.C.Vasu, 1997

(iii) वीरवीर्योच (A 6.2.120)

After सु *bv* in the vedic the words वीर and वीर्य have acture on the first syllable. (Trans., S.C. Vasu, 1997)

*CHAPTER - 5*

# KṚT AND SAMĀSĀNTODĀTTA

The kṛt *pratyaya-s* are primary suffixes that are involved in the formation of verbal nouns. *A* 3 deals with kṛt suffixation. A detailed survey of kṛt *pratyaya* and the related accentuation has been dealt with extensively by M.D. Balasubramaniam. In his thesis, he clearly distinguishes the typology of accent based on the *IT* and non *IT* endings of the various types of kṛt suffix. Given the variety of *anubandha-s* that are dropped off, it would be near impossible to present a uniform picture of "regular" kṛt suffixation and subsequent accentuation.

"As a matter of fact he states that accentuation, phonologically ard morphologically conditioned changes and other grammatical processes (as substitutions) are dealt with in Chapters 6 to 8 of the *A,* while he *P* exhaustively deals with the kṛt suffixation in Chapter 3".[1]

## 5.1 The Structure of kṛt *pratyaya-s (KP-s)*

M.D.Balasubrahmamam distributes 52 bound morphemes which *P* distributes in 128 primary suffixes,[2] as

1. accent *IT-s*
2. non accent *IT-s*
3. with accent and non accent *IT-s*
4. *IT* - less elements.

"The structure of a Pāṇinīa *KP* is such that the linkage of accent *IT-s* to bound morphemes is seen in the initial and final positions of *pratyaya-s* and non accent *IT-s* in the initial, penultimate and final positions of *pratyaya-s*".

A careful reading of M.D.Balasubrahmaniam's thesis provides the analysis of kṛt accentuation, the full details of which are beyond the scope of this chapter. His opinions are referred to only in those instances where they throw light on the contents of this chapter.

## 5.2 Scope of this Chapter

The primary focus in this chapter is on

1. defining the relations between kṛt and *samasontodātta*
2. the subsequent role of kṛt suffixation in compound accentuation as in *upapada* compounds.
3. The description of the *sūtra* गतिकारकोपपदात् कृत् (*A* 6.2.139)

## 5.3 Definition of the *sūtra gatikāraka-upapadāt kṛt* (*A* 6.2.139)

"In a *tp,* the original accent is retained when suffix is added at the end of a compound".

### 5.3.1 *kāraka* and *samāsāntodātta*

The *pūrvapadaprakṛtisvara,* the udātta is preserved in the illustration. A valid objection could be that which questions the need for the inclusion of the term कृत्. It could be argued that antecedent to *A* 6.2.139 it has already been pointed out by *P* that a *tp* which takes kṛt retains its original accent. Why then the redundancy ? Will A 6.1.139 be a *sūtra* of अतिव्याप्ति ? One has to go back into the *Mbh* for the answers.

In explaining the purpose of including the terms गति, कारक and उपपद in the *sūtra* there is a debate as to whether the illustration provided (by Patañjali) परमकारकम् is in fact कारकवाची at all. The objection could be whether the latter can be exemplified in such examples as शोभन कारकम्, परम कारकम्. Patañjali however establishes the validity of the examples here, but ascribes to it a qualifier -qualified relationship. Both Kaiyaṭa and Nāgeśa seem to concur with the fact that परमकारकम् is exemplifying a कारक relation but each expresses his opinion rather distinctly.

Kaiyaṭa questions the real difference between the counter examples and परमकारकम्. He seems to agree with Patañjali's opinion that 'परम' acts as qualifier rather than following a strict syntactic relation (as a कारकवाची should)

**एवं च तद्विशेषणमपि परमशब्द कारकवाची न भवति इति प्रति उदाहरणम्।**

He rules out the possibility that such formations as देवदत्तकारकम् are illustrations of कारक relations. He argues that परम is not a क्रियाविशेषण but rather a कर्म कारक which governs a substance (द्रव्य). Thus he establishes the compound to be a co-ordinate compound (*samānādh ikaraṇa).*

**कृदन्ता हि क्रियायोग्यताविष्टद्रव्यवाचिनः, न तूद्भुतां कारकतां प्रतिपादयन्ति। परममित्येतच्च न करोति क्रियाविशेषणम्, यतः कर्मकारकमेतत्स्यात् अपि तु द्रव्यविशेषणम्। तथा च समानाधिकरण समास उपपद्यते।**

To review Kaiyaṭa's initial comment

**यथा सम्प्रदानादयः शब्दाः न कारकरूपतां पतिपादयन्ति, तथा कारकशब्दोऽपि। तत् उत्तम-स्वशब्दैः अभिधाने तु सधर्मो नाभिधीयते। विभक्तयादिभिः एव असौ उपकारः प्रतीयते।।**[4]

Nāgeśa's comments center around these observations and in a manner unique to his style, he analyzes the compound (परमकारकम्) in terms of शक्ति denotative case. He explains the above verse in terms of शब्दशक्तिभाव. In his view the first member conveys the interdependence of the components of a compound.

**शब्दशक्तिस्वभाव्यादिति भावः। आदिशब्दो अत्र-आश्रयवाची विभक्तरूपैः आश्रयैः वाचकैः इत्यर्थः ।।**

### 5.4 kṛt and *samāsāntodātta*

In the following section of the *Mbh* regarding the purpose of including an objection provides two examples which obviate the purpose of *kṛt* occurence. Also, the question is when *gati* has been included in *A* 6.2.139 why is kṛt repeated as a distinct term. The explanation is that a verbal root can take only one of two *pratyaya-s,* a conjugational तिङ् or a कृत्.

*vārttika* 1

गत्यादिभ्य प्रकृतिस्वरत्वे
कृद्ग्रहणानर्थक्यमन्यस्योत्तरपदस्याभावात् ।

The discussion revolves around the relevance of including the term कृत् in the *sūtra A* 6.2.139 when the *prakṛtisvara* is already got by the mention of गति and कारक and उपपद. The explanation is that a verbal root (धातु) can take two types of suffixes - a conjugational suffix (तिङ्) or formative suffixes like कृत्. Kṛt can occur in a *samāsa* while the other cannot; therefore the occurence of kṛt is unique to the end of the compound.

तत्रान्तरेण कृद्ग्रहणं कृतः एव भविष्यति।

Hence the examples

निष्कौशाम्बिः निर्वाराणसि

are justified in their purpose of exemplifying the affixation of kṛt.

The relations between kṛt and *kāraka, gati* and *upapada* are explained by Kaiyaṭa. By the property of expressing 'Action', M.D.Balasubrahmaniam has succinctly distributed kṛt into *Ag. N* and *Ac. N* , i.e Action noun and Agent noun- kṛt suffixes occur at the *uttarapada* of the compound, similarly kṛt occurs in an *upapada* compound as well.

Nāgeśa points out that, in some usages of the vedic, even तिङ् occurs at the end of a compound. On the purpose of kṛt (to obviate तिङ् at the end) he says :

तिङन्तस्य तत् उत्तरपदत्वासंभवः, केवलधातोश्च तत्त्वासंभवोऽतः कृदन्तग्रहणमितिभावः।

Kātyāyana tries to point out the purpose of including kṛt as a term in the *sūtra,* in the following *vārttika.*

*vārttika* 2

कृत्प्रकृतौ वा गतित्वादधिकार्यं कृद्ग्रहणम् ।

In the *Mbh,* Patañjali opines that the purpose of kṛt is in its relation to the nucleus. This aspect of kṛt suffixation is also referred in M.D. Balasubrahmaniam's thesis. Here, Patañjali maintains that the nucleus is the धातु and कृत् is the suffix that operates on the धातु in the sense of action (क्रियायोग). The illustrations he provides are प्रणी: and उन्नी: He points out counter illustrations in प्रणायक: & उनायक:

It would be profitable to look at Kaiyaṭa's comments in this regard. Wherever the kṛt occurs in the relation of *dhātu* and *pratyaya* the original *prakṛtisvara* is retained. Otherwise the *uttarapada* carries the *svara.* With respect to प्रणी: Kaiyaṭa feels that it is *kṛtsvara* as an *apavāda* to *avyayasvara.*

Nāgeśa feels that it is due to the *'nityasambandha'* of *dhātu* and *pratyaya* that प्रणी: is possible and not प्रणायक:.

However, he feels that the *svara* of प्रणी: is *samāsāntodātta* (an *avyayasvara).* This difference in opinion is possible only due to the phrasing of 'वा' in the *vārttika,* which allows for option.

What follows in a short dialectic is an attack on the discussion of the inclusion of kṛt in the *sūtra*. The objection presented is that the action accomplished is not carried forth by कृत् but rather by the धातु itself.

In what is titled as the refutation of the purpose of the *vārttika* the argument goes back and forth between Patañjali and the objector. Concisely, the objector feels that since the purpose of "action" has already been accomplished by the mention of *gati* in the *sūtra* there really is little purpose served by the inclusion of the term कृत्.

In the final section dealing with the inclusion of kṛt as a "distinct" term, Patañjali has the following to say that it is for the sake of distinctiveness that कृत् is employed as a term in the *sūtra,*

"एषः अपि हि कर्तृविशिष्टस्यैव" as in the illustration

There is also a debate as to whether the inclusion of प्रभवनम् कृत् in the *sūtra* leads to a state of अतिव्याप्ति or अव्याप्ति. If कृत् is strictly to be grasped it is pointed out that some of the vedic expressions such as प्रपचतितराम्, प्रजल्पतितराम् are not possible, yet, they are found. Patañjali counters that the function of कृत् is in conveying भाव (impersonal passive) by expression and hence denotes substance *and* action.

**कृदभिहितो भावो द्रव्यवद्भवति क्रियावदपीति।**

Kaiyaṭa demonstrates the formation of a word such as प्रपचतितराम्, a compound after प्र शब्दः By A 6.2.139 when a *gati* and kṛt go to form a *samāsa* then the ending taken is सुप् and not kṛt in the compound.

**तेन तद्धितान्तेनापि सुबुत्पत्तेः समास प्रवर्वते।**

With respect to the accent observed in this *sūtra,* Kaiyaṭa feels that the term kṛt does not directly contribute to the *prakṛtisvara* but rather is employed for distinctiveness.

### 5.4.1 The Relationship of kṛt and Other *pratyaya-s* in a *samāsa* in their Contribution to Accent.

### 5.4.1.1 The Comment of the *Pradīpa* - Kaiyaṭa

Kaiyaṭa expresses the objector's view (paraphrased under *vārttika 2)* that where *sup* occurs at the end of a compound, kṛt is not seen. Therefore, by kṛt affixation, accent is not brought about.[5]

#### 5.4.1.1.1. *kṛt* and Nucleus

*kṛt* according to Kaiyaṭa conveys भाव in this case and as such is inter-related to *suffix, dravya, liṅga, saṁkhyā.*

#### 5.4.1.1.2. What is meant by *dravya* ?

Just as the substance of a pot, as an object is conveyed by the word घट, and conveys gender, number and the sense of "object", the word "पाक" conveys the भाव (impersonal action) of words under पाकादि the sense of baking or cooking or maturing. Here, the suffix conveys a sense of action as in a *upapada*. Kaiyaṭa's view therefore is that कृत् is included to obviate अव्याप्ति:

**तदेवमव्याप्तिप्रसङ्गात् प्रत्याख्यातं कृद्ग्रहणम् ।**

### 5.4.1.2 The Comment of the *Udyota* - Nāgeśa

According to Nāgeśa, the term 'प्रकृत्या' does not mean that the connotation of क्रिया as action alone is conveyed.[6] The relation of कृत् (accent) when the क्त (past passive participle) is also found in the compound, is also cited by Nāgeśa. The conditioning of accent by the क्त particle is treated separately in Chapter 6. He argues that in the examples provided by the objector (i.e. प्रपचतिदे: etc) the purpose is to illustrate the presence of उदात्त due to कुगति and सुप्सुपा. In response to how a verbal ending is affixed in the vedic, Nāgeśa points out that there is contradiction to the fact that there is no point or meaning to the affixation of तिङ् if this usage did not appear in the *Veda*.

Regarding the purpose of kṛt affixation Nāgeśa says

**तस्मात्क्रियाविशेषणकबोधकजनकेनापि समासे स्वरप्रवृत्यर्थ कृद्ग्रहणम्।**

Nāgeśa feels that the inclusion of kṛt is not just to convey a sense of distinctiveness (as Patañjali and Kaiyaṭa feel) but also to convey a sense of action. He concludes his discussion

**................ एवं व्याख्याने प्रभवनम् इत्यत्रैव क्रियावाचकत्वादत्र तुमुन्वत्स्वरः स्यादिति सर्वत्र स्वरप्रवृत्त्यर्थं कृद्ग्रहणमावश्यकं स्यादिति दिक्.**

### 5.5 A Review of the *sūtra-s* Delineating kṛt Suffix with Respect to Accentuation of Compounds.

A 6.2.2 - *tp* and kṛt - *tatpuruṣe tulyārtha....*

*A* 6.2.50 - *gati* and debars kṛt - *tādau ca niti kṛtyatau*

*A* 6.2.51 - debars kṛt - *tavai cāntaś ca yugapat*

*A* 6.2.75 - kṛt *ādyudātta* - *aṇi niyukte*

*A* 6.2.76 - kṛt - *pūrvapada ādyudātta* - *śilpini cākṛjñaḥ*

*A* 6.2.77 - *kṛt* and *upapada* - *samjñāyām ca*

*A* 6.2.79 - *ṇini*

*A* 6.2.139 - *kṛt, upapada, gati* - *gatikāraka upapadāt kṛt*

*A* 6.2.157 - kṛt and nañ - *ackāvaśaktau*

*A* 6.2.158 - kṛt and nañ - *ākrośe ca*

*A* 6.2.160 - kṛt and nañ - *kṛtyokaṣṇuccārvādayaś ca*

*A* 6.2.161 - kṛt and nañ - *vibhāṣā tṛnnannatīkṣṇaśuciṣu*

A further review of *gati* and kṛt is provided by *A* 6.2.50 in the light of the *Mbh.* Translations of *sūtra-s* are provided from S.C. Vasu, 1997.

### 5.5.1 तादौ च निति कृत्यतौ *(A 6.2.50)*

Here, the difference is established by the observation that a *gati* (such as प्र) retains its original accent before कृत् affixes that are निति. Kātyāyana's *vārttika* can be exemplified by the use of augment इट् when न् is final, e.g.

प्रकर्ता (तृन्)

प्रकर्तुम् (तृमुन्)

प्रकृतिः (क्तिन्)

प्रजल्पाकः (षाकन्)

Counter e.g.

आगन्तु *(Uṇādi* affix तुन्)

### 5.5.2. अणि नियुक्ते 6.2.75)

In a compound (verbal derivative) when the second member of which is a word ending in the kṛt affix - अण्, the acute is on the first syllable.

e.g.

छत्रधारः तूणींधारः कमण्डलुग्राहः, भृङ्गारधारः

### 5.5.3 शिल्पिनि चाकृञः (A 6.2.76)

The *sūtra* observes the semantic conditioning of kṛt on accent in compounds. Explicitly it states that when a compound indicates the term a "professional man" but debars the कार as the second term of the compound, then the acute is on the first syllable of the word, when the अण् affix is on the second term.

e.g.

तन्तुवायः, वालवायः

counter e.g.

कुम्भकारः, अयस्कारः

### 5.5.4 संज्ञायां च *(A 6.2.77)*

Here too the semantic basis for the affixation of kṛt in a *upapada* is seen. When the compound ends in अण् affix denoting a 'name' the acute falls on the first syllable. But not when the second term is 'कार'

e.g.

तुन्तुवायः, वालवायः,

counter e.g.

रथकार

### 5.5.5 णिनि (A 6.2.79)

When a compound has ṇini (a kṛt affix) on the final, it has acute on the first syllable of the first member

e.g.

पुष्पहारिन्, फलहारिन्, पर्णहारिन्

## 5.6 Relationship of kṛt and nañ Particle

### 5.6.1 अच्कावशक्तौ *(A* 6.2.157)

When a compound should convey the sense "not capable" and the word formed with the kṛt affix अच् and क is preceded by a nañ (नञ्) then the accent is on the final.

e.g.

**अपचः, अजयः, अनठः, अविक्षिपः**

Here the counter examples provide explanation for the semantic basis of accentuation.

counter e.g.

अपचः दीक्षितः

Here the दीक्षित does not cook not for a lack of competence but due to constraints of vows.

**5.6.2 आक्रोशे च (A 6.2.158)**

The above conditions of morphological formation are observed to cause a final in a compound when the overall sense conveys abuse (with the usage of that particular word)

e.g.

**अपचोऽयं जाल्मः**

**5.6.3 कृत्योकेष्णुच्चार्वादयश्च *(A 6.2.160)***

Similarly when कृत्य affixes by (उक, इष्णुच्) and terms चारु follow a नञ् the compound has *antodātta*.

कृत्या - अकर्त्तव्यम्

उक - अनागामुकम्

इष्णुच् - अनलङ्करिष्णुः

चारु - अचारुः

**5.6.4 विभाषा तृन्नन्नतीक्ष्णशुचिषु *(A 6.2.161)***

A semantic basis (where the words अन्न, तीक्ष्ण and शुचि) are formed with the affix तृन् and after the negative particle is seen in the following instances are

तृन् - अकर्त्ता or अकर्त्ता.

अन्न - अनन्नम् or अनन्नम्.

A study of the *sūtra-s* regarding कृत् and accentuation

reveals a complexity of networks. Kṛt is linked to the devolution of *gati,* to *prakṛtisvara* and to the negative morpheme, *nañ* . *Kṛt* accentuation in compounds is seen to be diverse.

Accent is conditioned by the type of compound; kṛt is conditioned by semantic or other morphological parameters.

## REFERENCES

1. Balasubrahmaniam, M.D. *"A System of Kṛt Accentuation in the Pāṇini and the Veda"*, Rashtriya Sanskrit Sansthan, Tirupati, 1981.
2. Ibid.
3. Vasu, S.C., *"The Astādhyāyī of Pāṇini"*, Motilal Banarsidass Publishing Ltd, New Delhi, reprinted 1997.
4. Pradīpa on Mbh on A 6.2.139.
5. Ibid.
6. Udyota on Mbh on A 6.2.139.

*CHAPTER - 6*

# KTA AND SAMĀSĀNTODĀTTA

The previous chapter dealt with the influence of kṛt as a morphological factor in accentuation of a compound, in particular, the *prakṛtisvara.* The succeeding Chapters 6,7 and 8 deal with the morphological and semantic influences on accentuation and the changes brought about in the same. The influence of *'kṛt'* and *'kta'* are treated purely as morphological factors influencing the *samāsasvara* in its complexity.

*'Kta* (क्त) is the *past passive participle* that in the cases of verbal compounds decides accentuation in a manner contrary to that of kṛt. Although the accentuation of a compound when *'kta'* is involved in word formation is defined as *antodātta,* in some cases, it is the *prakṛtisvara* that is retained when *'kta'* is involved in the formation of a compound, if *vibhakti* also regulates accentuation.

The following table is an encapsulation of the relations of *'kta'* to other morphological and semantic factors on compound accentuation.

**6.1 Past Passive Participle 'क्त' and *samāsāntodātta* :**

| ***sūtra* number** | **Relation described** | **Nature of Accent** |
|---|---|---|
| A 6.2.45 | *vibhakti* and *kta* (चतुर्थी) | *pūrvapadaprakṛtisvara* |
| A 6.2.46 | *vibhakti* and *kta* (चतुर्थी) | *pūrvapadaprakṛtisvara* |
| A 6.2.47 | *vibhakti* and *kta* (द्वितीया) | *pūrvapadaprakṛtisvara* |

| | | |
|---|---|---|
| A 6.2.48 | *vibhakti* and *kta* (तृतीया) | *pūrvapadaprakṛtisvara* |
| A 6.2.49 | *gati* and *kta* | *prakṛtisvara* |
| A 6.2.61 | *kta* and *sūtra* | *prakṛtisvara* (optional) |
| A 6.2.110 | *kta* in *bv* | *antodātta* (last syllable) |
| A 6.2.145 | *kta* in a compound | *antodātta* |
| A 6.2.146 | *gati kāraka upapada* and *kta* | *antodātta* |
| A 6.2.147 | *kta* ending | *antodātta* |
| A 6.2.149 | *kta* (semantic influence) | *antodātta* |

In considering the descriptions of each of these *sūtra-s* separately, the inter related complexity of morphological *(kṛt, kta* and *nañ )* and semantic *(naṃ, vibhakti)* influences on accentuation of compounds is revealed. In this chapter, the influence of *kta* as a morphological influence on accentuation is considered. Translations of the *sūtra-s* are provided from S.C. Vasu,1997.

## 6.2 An Elaboration of the *sūtra-s*

### 6.2.1 Relationship of *kta* and *vibhakti*

In these instances are seen the cases where विभक्ति acts as a semantic influence and क्त as a morphological element. However, it is judicious to comprehend the relationship as a whole than one in isolation from the other.

#### 6.2.1.1 *dvitīyā* and *kta*

This relation is described by the *sūtra* as follows :

अहीने द्वितीया A 6.2.47 (which also regulates accent in कष्टंश्रित: refer-Chapter 1).

Before a *past passive participle* in *'kta'* a word ending in the accusative case retains its accent, when it does not mean a separation.

This *sūtra* describes a semantic influence of *vibhakti* and the morphological influence of *kta* on *samāsa.*

**6.2.1.2 *tṛtīyā* and *kta***

The *sūtra A* 6.2.48 describes the combined influence of semantic conditions such as *tṛtīya* and *kta* of morphological influence on accentuation of compounds.

तृतीया कर्मणि (A 6.7.48)

A word ending in an instrumental case retains its accent, before the past participle in *kta,* when it has passive significance.

**6.2.1.3 *caturthī* and *kta***

*P* in two definitive *sūtra-s* relates the semantic motive of *caturthī* which retains the *pūrvapadaprakṛtisvara.*

**6.2.1.3.1 क्तेच (*A* 6.2.45)**

The first member in the *dative* case retains its accent before a *past participle* in *kta.*

e.g. गोहितम्

**6.2.1.3.2 कर्मधारयेऽनिष्ठा *(A* 6.2.46)**

Before a past participle in *kta,* the first member, when it is not a past participle, retains its original accent in a *karmadhāraya* compound.

e.g. पूगकृताः, ऊककृताः

**6.2.2 The Relationship of *gati* and *kta***

The influence of *gati* in a verbal compound was seen in Chapter 5. Here the illustration of the inter-related influence of gati and kta is treated.

**6.2.2.1 गतिरनन्तरः *(A* 6.2.49)**

A word called *gati (A.* 1.4.60), when standing immediately before a participle in *kta* having a passive significance, retains its accent.

e.g. प्रकृतः, प्रहृतः

Here, either the *samāsāntodātta* (*A* 6.1.223), *avyayasvara* (*A* 6.2.2) or *uttarapada prakṛtisvara* (*A* 6.2.139 and 4 6.2.144) prevails as per the influence of *gati* or *kta*.

### 6.2.3 Semantic Influence and *kta*

In three prominent instances *P* highlights the nature by which 'sense' influences accent when *kta* is involved in *samāsa* formation.

#### 6.2.3.1 *kta* and Sense

(i) क्ते नित्यार्थे (A 6.2.61)

When a word has the sense of *"always"* it retains optionally its accent before *kta*.

S.C. Vasu also points out that in such illustrations as those that follow the *accusative* case *kta* acts as a semantic influence on compound word formation.

e.g. नित्यंप्रहसित:, नित्यप्रहसित:

(ii) सूपमानात् क्तः (A 6.2.145)

The participle in क्त has acute on the final when it is preceded by सु or by a word with which the second member is compounded.

e.g. सुकृतम्, सुभुक्तम्

Here, the accent is *antodātta*.

#### 6.2.3.2 Semantic Motivation and *kta*

इथंभूतेन कृतमिति (*A* 6.2.149)

The participle in *kta* has acute on the final when the compound denotes 'done by one in such a condition'.

Here it is the sense of the term इत्थंभूत (being in such a condition) that serves to contribute to *antodātta* along with *kta* which is used in word formation.

e.g. सुप्तप्रलपितम्

### 6.2.4 *kta* in a *bv*

**निष्टोपसर्गपूर्वमन्यतरस्याम् (A 6.2.110)**

In a *bv* a participle in *kta* preceded by a *preposition,* standing as the first member of the compound, has *antodātta.*

e.g. प्रधौतमुख:

### 6.2.5 *kta* Ending in a *samāsa*

प्रवृद्धादीनं च (*A* 6.2.147)

The words and others ending in *kta* have acute on the final.

e.g. प्रवृद्धं यानम्, प्रवृद्धो वृषल:

Here although the sense of the term does not directly dictate the sense of the compound and its accent, the formation of the compound is such that it brings about *antodātta.*

In these five subsections one finds that the accentuation of *samāsa* is conditioned by the presence of *kta.* In combination with *vibhakti* it brings about *prakṛtisvara.* When *gati, kāraka* or *upapada* are involved *kta* brings about *antodātta* reversing the influence of kṛt which naturally restores *prakṛtisvara.*

Semantic influences together with *kta* bring about *antodātta* in contrast to the effect of *vibhakti.*

*CHAPTER - 7*

# NAÑ AND SAMĀSĀNTODĀTTA

The Scope of this Chapter :

The relationship of नञ् to accentuation of nañ *-bv-s* is a complex one; it is at one level morphological and at a deeper level, semantic. नञ् as a particle contributes morphologically to the formation of a compound and as a *sememe* to the semantic effects of accentuation.[1] Thus, नञ् affects accentuation in two ways but the effect is bringing about *samāsāntodātta*.

## 7.1 The Relations of the Negative Particle and *samāsāntodātta*

| | | |
|---|---|---|
| *A* 6.2.116 | *bv, nañ* (जर, मर, मित्र, मृत) | antodātta |
| *A* 6.2.155 | *taddhita* and *nañ* | antodātta |
| *A* 6.2.156 | *taddhita* and *nañ* | antodātta |
| *A* 6.2.157 | *kṛt* and *nañ* | antodātta |
| *A* 6.2.158 | *kṛt* and *nañ* | antodātta |
| *A* 6.2.159 | sense and *nañ* | antodātta |
| *A* 6.2.160 | *kṛtya* and *nañ* | antodātta |
| *A* 6.2.161 | sense and *nañ* | antodātta |
| *A* 6.2.172 | nañ in *bv* | antodātta |
| *A* 6.2.173 | *nañ* in *bv* | accent on syllable before last vowel. |
| *A* 6.2.174 | nañ in *bv* | *svara* on syllable before the last vowel. |

Translations of the *sūtra-s* are provided from S.C. Vasu,1997.

## 7.2 Relations of Morphemes with *nañ*

### 7.2.1 *taddhita* and *nañ*

Two *sūtra-s* define the relationship of affixes such as *taddhita-s* to nañ as a negative particle or *negative morpheme.* In, a compound such as a *nañ -bv* as अमाष: seen in Chapter 3 the effect of including नञ् in the morphology serves to bring about *samāsāttodātta,* obviating the *prakṛtisvara* of *bv.* This is treated in detail in subsections 7.2.4 *(nan* in *bv).* In the previous tabulation, the complexity of interactions of morphemes *(taddhita, kṛt* and *kṛtya)* and sense (meaning conditions to *nañ* ) is highlighted.

#### 7.2.1.1 *taddhita* and nañ in a *samāsa*

*A* 6.2.155 and *A* 6.2.156 are two *sūtra-s* that describe the *samāsāntodātta* brought about when *taddhita-s* are involved in compound word formation.

#### 7.2.1.1.1 नञो गुणप्रतिषेधे संपाद्यर्हहितालमर्थास्तसिद्धताः (A 6.2.155)

When nañ negates the sense (of "fitted for that." "deserving that", "good for that", "capable to effect that") of the *taddhita* affixes, the accentuation of the *samāsa* is final.

e.g. अकार्णवेष्टकिकम्

#### 7.2.1.2 ययतोश्चातदर्थे (A 6.2.156)

When *taddhita* affixes य and यत् are not used in the sense of "useful for that" and have नञ् negating that particular sense, then the *samāsa* has *antodātta.*

**e.g.** अपाश्या:

### 7.2.2. kṛt and nañ in a *samāsa*

#### 7.2.2.1 अच्कावशक्तौ *(A 6.2.157)*

When नञ् negates and gives the meaning of 'not capable'

then the word which is formed by kṛt affixes अच् and क has *antodātta samāsāntodātta* brought about when *taddhita-s* are involved in compound word formation.

**7.2.2. kṛt and nañ in a *samāsa***

**7.2.2.1 अच्कावशक्तौ *(A 6.2.157)***

When नञ् negates and gives the meaning of 'not capable' then the word which is formed by kṛt affixes अच् and क has *antodātta.*

e.g. अपचः

**7.2.2.2 आक्रोशे च *(A 6.2.158)***

Similar to the conditions laid down in *A* 6.2.157, when nañ negates the *sense* of abuse (someone abuses using that word) then the accent is *samāsāntodātta.*

e.g. अपचोऽयं जाल्मः

Vasu points out that it is only avarice that makes the fellow wanting pay before he will work and not incompetence.

**7.2.2.3 कृत्योकेष्णुच्चार्वादयश्च (A 6.2.160)**

When the affixes are *kṛtya* affixes in words such as and इष्णुच and चारु then too *samāsāntodātta* comes about.

e.g. अकर्त्तव्यम्

**7.2.3 nañ Conditions Meaning**

**7.2.3.1 संज्ञायाम् *(A 6.2.159)***

When abuse is meant, a word preceded by नञ् has acute on the final, in denoting a name.

e.g. अदेवदत्तः

**7.2.3.2 विभाषा तृन्नन्नतीक्ष्णशुचिषु *(A 6.2.161)***

After the negative particle, the final of the following is optionally acute - a word formed with the affix तृन् and the words अन्न, तीक्ष्ण and शुचि".

e.g. अकर्त्ता

### 7.2.4 nañ -*bv*

नञ् सुभ्याम् (*A* 6.2.172)

कपि पूर्वम् (A 6.2.173)

ह्रस्वान्ते अन्त्यात्पूर्वम् (A 6.2.174)

Taken together, these three *sūtra-s* reflect *P's* observations on accentuation in nañ -*bv*. The background of *A* 6.2.172 was already discussed in Chapter 3 as an exception to *A* 6.2.1. By *A* 6.2.1 one observes *pūrvapadaprakṛtisvara* in a *samāsa*. However, by नञ्सुभ्याम् *samāsāntodātta* is obtained, Hence it defines *apavāda-s* to 1 6.2.1. In chapter 2 it was elaborated under and *bv* that 6v formed by नञ् and सु will have *samasāntodātta* and when the compound ends in a light vowel, then the acute falls on the syllable before the last member (the conditions being that the *bv* is preceded by नञ् or सु and *-kap* is added).

In a summary of this subsection the observations are that nañ indisputably exerts its influence as a semantic factor negating the "sense" of the affix and also as a determining factor in deciding the *samāsāntodātta*. In unequivocally deciding the accentuation as *samāsāntodātta* the nañ particle is seen to act by the principle of *satiśiṣṭa* elaborated in Chapter 3. Thus the effect of nañ is stronger than *vibhakti,* and in the case of nañ b*v-s* is an *apavāda* to *A* 6.2.1.

## REFERENCE

1. It is thought that the negative particle is semantic. However the ramifications of the semantic basis of नञ् is detailed by Caturvedi in his work on Bhartṛhari's Vṛttisamuddeśa. Using the example अब्राह्मण provided in the Mbh he argues that Bhartṛhari maintains नञ् is only indicative and not expressive contrary to Patanjali's claim that the negative particle नञ् is semantic.
For an extensive discussion on the illustration of see Caturvedi 2001.

*CHAPTER - 8*

# VIBHAKTI AND SAMĀSĀNTODĀTTA

The relationship of the case-affix *(vibhakti)* to the *samasānta* is through the relation of its accent, the *samāsāntodātta.* In the section regarding kṛt and *samāsāntodātta,* there was already a mention of *kāraka* relations to *samāsāntodātta.* However, while *kāraka* was referred to in the perspective of object-oriented activity there, here the emphasis is on the casal relations to accent on a compound.

The answer to the question "Why should this be taken up for study ?" lies partly in the fact that *vibhakti lopa* is a crucial step in the formation of a compound. The next question is then, whether the *vibhakti* influences the semantic motivation for accent. /' in his observations regarding compound accentuation *(vibhakti)* and casal definitions points out those instances where such an influence over accentuation does take place.

However, an observation of those *sūtra-s* of *P* that requires a description of specific instances of casal relations to accentuation should in fact be preceded by an explanation of the *sūtra* तिसृभ्यो जसः from the *6th adhyāya 1st pāda* of the *A.* It is a *sūtra* that is directly relevant to the discussion on *vibhaktyudātta* of a *samāsa.*

## 8.1 Relations between *vibhakti* and *udātta*

### 8.1.1 Nominative Casal Affix ( जसि )

#### 8.1.1.1 तिसृभ्यो जस : *(A 6.1.166)*

The *sūtra* तिसृभ्यो जसः is a discussion centered around the interplay of the effects of word, accent, and number. Taking as an example the number "three" (which can be declined in the plural only), Kaiyaṭa in the *vibhaktyudāttādhikaraṇam* discusses the reasons for choosing the same (word) to provide an illustration to the relations between casal - affix and *udātta.*

Kaiyaṭa "अर्थगतं बहुत्वशब्दे आरोप्य बहुवचननिर्देशः। अन्तोदात्तस्य त्रिशब्दस्य स्थाने तिसृशब्द आदेशः स्थानिवद्भवादन्तोदात्तः"

"In the instances where the meaning is conveyed as plurality one can only resort to बहुवचन. The *antodātta* of ति does not take root here, rather the अन्तोदात्त comes about due to an exception to अनुदात्त and by *sthānivadbhāva*"[1]

In the objection that follows, the objector makes a point that the property of accentuation of जसः (treated as a casal - affix here) cannot be extended to such nominal bases which are एकवचन or द्विवचन

To counter this objection, an illustration is given तिसृका which employs तिसृ but in the sense of एकवचन. In the example Patañjali elaborates that there is contradiction to नित्स्वर *(nitsvara)* and by अनुदात्तौ सुप्पितौ, (A 3.1.4) तिसृस्वर is retained.

However, in the discussion where the objector points out that it is the सुप् affixed accent that is contradicted and not the नित्स्वर *(nitsvara),* it is with much ambivalence that Patañjali agrees to this but with some hesistation.

The discussion that follows has to be logically on the accent of *sup* affix (the सुप्) जस्. Patañjali provides the examples अतितिस्रौ and अतितिस्रः. This is regarded as the function of the casal affix (जस्प्रयोजनम्). Let us take up Kaiyaṭa's argument here. He maintains that the विभक्ति-उदात्त of a word as अतितिस्रौ comes about by the contradiction of *antodātta,* but it comes about due to the maxim उत्तरकृत्पद and अतेर्धातुलोप इति वक्तव्यम्. Thus we see here an exertion of the influence of a कृत्-पद as well as ध ातुलोप in bringing about an absence of *antodātta* . By the *sūtra* mentioned in the reference *svarita* is brought about.

In the examples अतितिस्रः, it (the उदात्त) is purely a product of the casal affix जसः according to Kaiyaṭa.

So far, the discussion on the *vibhaktisvara* centered around the direct relations between *svara* and *vibhakti* and the deviances from the norm. Now *P* introduces a semantic element in the *A* by the *sūtra* चतुरः शसि where a पद acts as a semantic condition influencing the nature of accent (casal - affix accent or *antodātta)*. Whether we can consider this to be a true example of semantic motivation (for *vibhakti-udātta)* is a moot point, a highly debatable one at that. Yet given the background of the discussion on तिसृभ्यो जसः, it is not illogical to at least deduce a certain degree of semantic conditioning in certain उदाहरण-s

### 8.1.2 Accent of the Accusative

चतुरः शसि (A 6.1.167)

The accent of the accusative plural case affix is defined by the *sūtra 'caturaḥ śasi'*[2]' Here, it is defined as the accent on the last syllable when the accusative plural affix follows the word चतुर्. चतुर्. has accute on the first; hence the form चतुर॑ः पश्य. Its feminine substitute चतसृ will also have acute on the first by *sthānivadbhāva.*

The word is चतसृ + शस् (=चतस्र + शस)

By *A* 6.1.167 the र् substitute of ऋ is considered to be स्थानिवद्भव.[3] Importantly, it prevents the *udātta* formation of अ of the त: ऋ doesn't take an accent and र् cannot. Hence the formation is चतस्रः पश्य.

Professor Böhtlingk places the accent thus -च॒तु॒रः Prof. Max Muller - च॒तु॒र॑ *S.C.* Vasu prefers the latter.

The *ākṣepa vārttika* explains the need for *vibhaktisvara* as "विभक्तिस्वरभावश्च हलादि ग्रहणात्". Patañjali answers the objector's query (कुतः) that the purpose of विभक्तिस्वर is for the sake of grasping हलादि (case endings beginning with the consonant). To justify this, he says यदयं षट्त्रिचतुर्भ्यो हलादि: (A 6.1.179).

इति हलादि ग्रहणं करोति तत् ज्ञापयत्याचार्य:।

In the succeeding *vārttika,*

आद्युदात्तनिपातने हि हलादि ग्रहणानर्थक्यम्,

the discussion centers around the fact that the need for accent of casal - affixes (beginning with consonants) is rendered useless when a *nipātanasvara* is present in the word. The objector feels that *nipātanasvara* contradicts the *vibhaktisvara.* However, Kaiyaṭa is of the view that *vibhaktisvara* dominates. Coming back to तिसृ शब्द after showing that षट् and चतुर् cannot be declined in either द्विवचन or एकवचन, Patañjali echoing the objector also points out that accent of जस् and शस् are rendered superfluous in तिसृ and चतुर् respectively. The reason provided by Patañjali is असर्वनामस्थानम् जसि is rendered superfluous.[4]

**असर्वनामस्थानम् इति वचनात् जसि न भवितव्यम् ।**

As far as शसि is concerned, the accent is governed by उदात्तयणो हल्पूर्वात् (A 6.1.174). By this *sūtra, udātta* is got. The *nipātanasvara* contradicts consonantal case affixation during the declension process. The *ajādi* case affixes are *asarvanāmasthāna.* This is the view of Patañjali. Kaiyaṭa feels that the mention of the term चतसृ is to remind one that the *vibhaktisvara* dominates.

**तत्र चतसृशब्दादेकस्माच्छस् - असर्वनाम्स्थानम् अजादि: विभक्ति इति। यदि च अत्र निपातनस्वर: स्यात् हलदिग्रहणमनर्थकं स्यात्।**

In the सिद्धान्तभाष्य as indicated in the introduction to this section, Patañjali categorically states that the accent of शसि is due to *sthānivadbhāva.* The विभक्तिस्वर in words such as चतुसृ comes about due to this principle.

**8.1.3 The Instrumental and Locative Cases.**

Instrumental and other case affixes are said to carry the

acute accent, so also a monosyllabic stem in locative plural. This is defined by सावेकाचस्तृतीयादिभिः विभक्तिः (A 6.1.168).[5]

Here, no special semantic conditions are mentioned. However, what is of concern to Patañjali is the need to distinguish सो as प्रथम-एकवचन or as सप्तमी बहुवचन. In the dialectic that follows Patañjali refers to the *sūtra* न गो वन्सावववर्ण *(A* 6.1.182).[6] This *sūtra* helps to distinguish between the accentual properties of nominative singular and locative plural, while the *sūtra* is rendered superfluous when प्रथमा-एकवचन comes into effect.

In the succeeding *vārttika-s Patañjali* explains

**सावेकाच उदात्तात्वे त्वनमदो प्रतिषेधः सिद्धं तु यस्मात् तृतीया-दिस्तस्याभावात्सौ**

In the plural of the locative, they have more than one syllable though in singular-locative their stem has one syllable- वाचौ, वाचः, as in त्वया and त्वयि (examples for the instrumental). When the stem (in locative plural) is monosyllabic the example could be राजसु

' The study of accents of individual case affixes has revealed the property of विभक्ति-उदात्त that counters अन्तोदात्त in words during the declensional process. Semantic conditions that put a constraint on this विभक्ति-उदात्त were also highlighted, indirectly connoting relation to the अन्तोदात्तः. The succeeding *sūtra-s* in *A* 6.2 tackle accentuation in समास and is best dealt with in the subsection dealing with the accentuation of compounds and विभक्ति-उदात्त.

## 8.2 *vibhakti - udātta* in a Compound

It has been demonstrated that the declensional case affixes carry an accent; also, in certain cases they are semantically conditioned by words such as तिसृ or चतुर् which convey number (or numerals). In this section of the *6th adhyāya 1st pāda* Patañjali introduces the concept of *udātta* (of the *vibhakti)* in a *samāsa*. As an introduction to the observations of the semantic underpinnings of in a *samāsa* (in *A* 6.2) he first discusses the nature of विमत्तयुदात्त in the *6th adhyāya 1st pāda* in terms of the accent of the case-affix in a *samāsa* a compound whose constituent meanings cannot be separated.

### 8.2.1 Case-affix, Accent and *nityasamāsa* :

The first inkling of the nature of accentuation (influenced by विभक्ति) in a *samāsa* is given in the *sūtra* -

**अन्तोदात्तादुत्तरपदादन्यतरस्यामनित्यसमासे** (A 6.1.169).[7]

The discussion provided in the *Mbh* is actually an extension of the observations on the inclusion of a vowel (carrying the accent) in a *samāsa*. The previous *sūtra (A* 6.1.168) was a discussion of the need to distinguish between nominative singular and locative plural which Patañjali distinguishes by the presence of an extended vowel in the locative plural forms.

Here, this 'एकाच्' is tied to the position of the accent in those compounds that are not नित्यसमास-s Patañjali provides the examples

शुनः, ऊर्क्श्वोर्क्,श्वोर्जा,श्वोर्ज

Thus though *vibhakti* - *udātta* is seen to be predominantly antithetical, contradictory to अन्तोदात्त, under this semantic condition only उत्तरपदग्रहाम् is possible. The inclusion of the vowel is regarded to be specific to the designation and formation of समास. Kaiyaṭa feels (with respect to समासविशेषणम्) that from the term अनित्यसमास in the *sūtra* one has to deduce the fact that it is सतिसप्तमी

### 6.3 *vibhaktyudātta* and *samāsa* -

### Semantic Conditioning of Accentuation in *samāsa*

The following table demonstrates the semantic conditioning of *samāsāsvara* due to the *vibhakti* of the compound.

| | | | |
|---|---|---|---|
| A 6.2.2 | *tp* | - | द्वितीया, तृतीया, सप्तमी |
| A 6.2.32 | *tp* | - | सप्तमी |
| A 6.2.43 | *tp* | - | चतुर्थी |
| A 6.2.44 | *tp* | - | चतुर्थी |
| A 6.2.45 | *tp* | - | चतुर्थी |
| A 6.2.47 | *tp* | - | द्वितीया |
| A 6.2.48 | *tp* | - | तृतीया |
| A 6.2.65 | *tp* | - | सप्तमी |
| A 6.2.134 | *tp* | - | षष्ठी |
| A 6.2.151 | *tp* | - | कारक relations |
| A 6.2.152 | *tp* | - | सप्तमी |
| A 6.2.153 | *tp* | - | तृतीया |

An attempt is made here to provide a detailed account of each विभक्ति that conditions the accent of the compound. Whereas the *sūtra* no.s were listed in their order of the A, below a group of *sūtra-s* that define a particular विभक्ति is grouped together. Translations of *sūtra-s* are provided from S.C. Vasu, 1997.

**8.3.1 *dvitīya* and Accentuation.**

The *tp* accent is conditioned by the second case (द्वितीया विभक्ति). In two *sūtra-s* P observes the following nature of accentuation.

**8.3.1.1 तत्पुरुषे**

**तुल्यार्थतृतीयासप्तम्युपमानाव्ययद्वितीयाकृत्याः । *(A 6.2.2)***

Here the *pūrvapadaprakṛtisvara* is retained by the conditions imposed on accentuation by the *vibhakti* of the compound (द्वितीया)

e.g. मुहूर्त्तसुखम्, मुहूर्तरमणीयम्, सर्वरात्रकल्याणी, सर्वरात्रशोभना

सर्वरात्र is formed by the *samāsānta* अच् and is finally accented.

**8.3.1.2 अहीने द्वितीया (A 6.2.47)**

Before a past participle in '*kta*' a word ending in the accusative case retains its accent, when it does not mean separation.

The common example for this *sūtra* is कष्टंश्रितः which is discussed in the context of महाकष्टंश्रितः Chapter 1. The semantic relationship of the accent and *vibhakti* were obvious from the *Samarthāhnika*.

Kātyāyana adds an observation that this *sūtra* does not apply when क्त has an *upasarga* attached.

e.g. सुखप्राप्तः, दुःखप्राप्तः

Both A 6.2.2 and A 6.2.47 define the retention of the *pūrvapadaprakṛtisvara* due to the semantic conditioning of the accusative case of the first member of the compound. The *sūtra* A 6.1.223 defines the *antodātta* of the *samāsa (samāsāntodātta)*. Semantic preconditions or morphological constraints (as *kṛt, gati, nan)* condition a *tp* to possess *pūrvapadaprakṛtisvara*. Here, this is a demonstration that *vibhakti* too acts as a semantic conditioning factor in the retention of *pūrvapadaprakṛtisvara*.

**8.3.2 *tṛtīyā* and Accentuation**

Four *sūtra-s* define the retention of *pūrvapadaprakṛtisvara* in a compound.

**8.3.2.1 तत्पुरुषे**

**तुल्यार्थतृतीयासप्तम्युपमानाव्ययद्वितीयाकृत्याः *(A.6.2.2)***

e.g. शङ्कुलाखंण्डः, किरिकांणः

**8.3.2.2 तृतीया कर्मणि (A 6.2.48)**

A word ending in an instrumental case retains its accent before the past participle in *'kta'* when it has passive meaning.

Interesting illustrations are the compounds महाराजहंतः and नखनिर्भिन्ना

महाराजहंत: *mahārāja* is formed by the *samāsanta* affix टच्, नखनिर्भिन्ना - *nakha* is formed by ख affix added to नह् *(Uṇādi.* v. 23) or it may be a *bv* नास्य खमस्ति = नख: formed by अच् (A 5.4.121).

**8.3.2.3. ऊनार्थकहलं तृतीयाया: (A 6.2.153)**

The acute falls on the final of words having the sense of ऊन and of कलह when they are second members in a compound provided by a term in the instrumental case.

It is important to note that the sematic conditioning occurs only due to the nature of the second member rather than the विभक्ति which is only mentioned for clarity.

This *sūtra* is an exception to विभक्ति-उदात्त and shows अन्तोदात्त, presumably due to the influence of the second member of the compound.

e.g. माषोनम्, कार्षापणोनम्

S.C. Vasu argues that the word अर्थ in the *sūtra* can be taken to mean synonyms of ऊन as well as the word अर्थ as a result of which, there would result, formations as : धान्यर्थ: as well.

**8.3.2.4 मिश्रं चानुपसर्गमसंधौ (A 6.2.154)**

The word मिश्र has acute on the final after an instrumental case, when it is not joined with any preposition and does not mean a contract or alliance. ,

This *sūtra* too is an exception to the विभक्ति-उदात्त of a compound. Here the second member conditions a final acute. Yet, the requirement of an instrumental case in the first member suggests the over bearing semantic condition imposed by विभक्ति in a *samāsa*.

e.g. गुडमिश्रा:, तिलमिश्रा:, सर्पिर्मिश्रा:

**8.3.3 *caturthī* and Accentuation**

**8.3.3.1 चतुर्थी तदर्थे (A 6.2.43)**

A word in the *dative* case as the first member retains its accent, when the second member expresses that which is suited to become the former(member).

**8.3.3.2 यूपदारू, कुण्डलहिरण्यम्**

The accent of यूप is ordained by *Uṇādi,* iii. 27 on प and is treated as a नित्. The word कुण्डल is formed by कल affix and treated as नित् *(Uṇādi,* i. 108).

**8.3.3.2 अर्थे *(A* 6.2.44)**

Before the word *'artha'* the first member in the *dative* retains its accent.

e.g. मात्रर्थम्, पित्रर्थम्

S.C. Vasu points out the difference between *A* 6.2.43 and *A* 6.2.44. The former like दारु and हिरण्य has not inherent in it the sense of adaptability while अर्थ means adapted. According to some, the making of two *sūtra-s,* one as अर्थ and the other as indicates that the former rule is applicable only to that compound where the material itself is changed into the substance of the first.

**8.3.3.3 क्तेच (A 6.2.45)**

The first member in the *dative* case retains its accent before a *past participle* in *kta.*

**e.g.** गोहितम्, मनुष्यहितम्, अश्वहितम्

From the above observations it is clear that the *caturthi vibhakti* conditions the accentuation of a compound making it *pūrvapadaprakṛitisvara* (an *apavāda* to *samāsāntodātta).*

**8.3.4 *sasthī* and Accentuation**

**8.3.4.1 चूर्णादीन्यप्राणिषष्ठचाः (A 6.2.134)**

The words चूर्ण and others in a *tp* have acute on the first syllable when the preceding word ends in a *genitive* and does not denote a living being.

e.g. मुद्गचूर्णम्, मसूरचूर्णम् but not मत्स्यचूर्णम् (first term being a living being) and परमचूर्णम् (where it is not *genitive).*

The other words are चूर्ण करिव, करिप, शकिन, शाकट, द्राक्षा, तूस्त, कुन्दम, दलप, चमसी, चक्कन, चौल.

In this *sūtra* the assumption (by *anuvṛtti)* is that the accent is *ādyudātta* of the first member. It is not a *prakṛtisvara.* Also this *sūtra* describes the casal nature of the first member *(genitive)* that acts as a conditioning factor in accentuation. Thus, this too is an instance of *apavāda* to *samāsāntodātta.*

### 8.3.5 *saptamī* and Accentuation

There are four *sūtra-s* that define the relationship of सप्तमी विभक्ति to accent. The first of this is A 6.2.2 which has already been discussed extensively in Chapter 3. The other three *sūtra-s* are examined below.

#### 8.3.5.1 सप्तमीहारिणौ धर्म्येऽहरणे (A 6.2.65)

The first member of a compound, if in the locative case denoting the name of the receiver of a tax has acute on the first syllable, when the second member is a word denoting 'what is lawful' but not when it is हरण.

e.g. स्तूपे-शाणः, मुकुटे-कार्षापणम्.

The word हरण is a kṛt formed word. By its exclusion in this *sūtra* it indicates that other kṛt formed words are हारि governed by this rule when preceded by a हारी denoting word; thus this *sūtra* supersedes the kṛt accent enjoined by A 6.2.139. To take note is the fact that by *anuvṛtti,* it is defined that the accent is *ādyudātta.* The term *prakṛtisvara* is avoided for the sake of clarity.

#### 8.3.5.2 सप्तम्याः पुण्यम् (A 6.2.152)

The word पुण्य has acute on the final when preceded by a noun in the locative case.

e.g. अध्ययनपुण्यम्, वेदपुण्यम्

By A 6.2.2 the first member would have preserved its accent, the present *sūtra* supercedes that and ordains *antodātta*. पुण्य is derived from *Uṇādi* affix यत् and would have retained its natural accent (A 6.1.213) and consequently get acute on the first syllabic by kṛt accent (A 6.2.139). But by this *sūtra* it gets *antodātta*.

**8.3.5.3 सप्तमी सिद्धशुष्कपक्वबन्धेष्वकालात् (A 6.2.32)**

A locative ending word, when it does not denote time, preserves its original accent, when followed by सिद्ध, शुष्क, पक्व & बन्ध in a compound.

e.g. **सांकाश्यसिद्धः, सांकाश्यसिद्धः**
**काम्पिल्यसिद्ध, काम्पिल्यसिद्धः**

The accent of *locative tp* (A 6.2.2) was debarred by kṛt accent taught in A 6.2.144.

A 6.2.32 (this *sūtra)* debars A 6.2.144 regarding kṛt accent and reordains *locative tp* when the kṛt words are सिद्ध and others.

## A BRIEF SUMMARY OF CHAPTER 8

(1) *A* 6.1.223 ordains *antodātta* in a *samāsa*.

(2) A 6.2.2 (an *apavāda* to A 6.1.223) ordains *pūrvapadaprakṛtisvara* in the instances where accusative, instrumental and locative condition the accent of the compound. Therefore there is no *antodātta* in these instances.

(3) In certain instances of *tṛtīyā vibhakti* it is the nature of the second member that determines accent. These instances are exceptions to *vibhaktyudātta*.

(4) *caturthi* is also seen to condition the accent as *pūrvapadaprakṛtisvara*.

(5) *P* makes no observations on *paṃcamī* in A 6.2.

(6) Regarding *ṣaṣṭhī* S.C. Vasu is careful to point out that *ādyudātta* (not necessarily the *prakṛtisvara)* is the accent of the first member of a compound. Yet, it brings about an *apavāda* to *antodātta.*

(7) By *A* 6.2.28 and *A* 6.2.32 *locative* ordains *prakṛtisvara* is a tp (*apavāda* to 6.1.223). By A 6.2.65 the first syllable of the first member carries the accent (*ādyudātta)*. By *A* 6.2.152 *locative* co-occurs with *antodātta.*

(8) From Chapter 3. and A 6.2.132 it is observed that nañ accent is stronger than *vibhakti* accent. From these observations one can ascertain that there exists a predominant semantic factor in accentuation in a compound. *Vibhaktyudātta* in most cases restores the *prakṛtisvara.* In those instances where homonymy is seen the *antodātta* is retained. But, in the latter observation too, it is the semantic propensity of a word (पद) that brings about accent.

To sum up, in the words of Macdonnell possessives and governing compounds accent the first member while determinatives (*karmadhāraya* and *tatpuruṣa)* and regularly formed co-ordinatives accent the last member (usually the final syllable).

## REFERENCES

1. स्थानिवद्भाव

   A 1.1.48 - A 1.1.57 deal with the designations of substitutions according to P. The exception to A 1.1.57 is svaravidhi and it is detailed under A 1.1.58 By this property exception to sthānivadbhāva is achieved.

2. चतुरः शसि (A 6.1.167)

   The word चतुर् followed by the accusative plural has accent on the last syllabic. (Trans.. S.C. Vasu, 1997)

3. Notes No. 1 (Chapter 8)

4. असर्वनामस्थानम्

   A 1.4.17 defines the asarvanāmasthāna.

5. सावेकाचस्तृतीयादिर्विभक्तिः (A 6.1.168)

   The case affixes of the Instrumental and of the cases that follow have acute acccent if the stem in locative plural is monosyllabic.(Trans. S.C. Vasu, 1997)

6. न गोश्वन्त्साववर्णराडङ्क्रुङ्कृदभ्यः (A 6.1.182)

   Rules from 6.1.168 downwards have no applicability after गो and श्वन् and words ending in them; nor after a stem which before the end of the nominative singular has अ and आ or after रज् or after a stem ending in क्रुञ्च् or कृत् (Trans., S.C. Vasu 1997)

7. अन्तोदात्तादुत्तरपदादन्यतरस्यामनित्यसमासे (A 6.1.169).

   The same case endings may optionally have accute accent, if the monosyllabic word stands at the end of a compound and has accute accent on the final when the compound can be easily unloosened. ( Trans., S.C. Vasu, 1997)

# CONCLUSION

The concluding remarks of this thesis are grouped under two separate headings.

**I. Observations**

**II. Summary and Discussion**

**I. Observations**

1. *Samāsānta* is defined as an *atyantasvārthika pratyaya* (a *taddhita)* which can undergo grammatical processes in compound word formation.
2. The nature of *samāsānta* is such that it carries a final acute *(samāsāntodātta)* on its indicatory letter (the *anubandha)*. The necessity for a variety of *samāsānta* is in keeping with the heterogenous nature of *anubandha*.
3. The four principal *sūtra-s* that govern accentuation of compounds are
   - *anudāttam padam ekavarjam (A* 6.1.158),
   - *samāsasya* (*A* 6.1.223),
   - *bahurvrīhau prakṛtyā pūrvapadam (A* 6.2.1),
   - *tatpuruṣe*

     *tulyārthatiyāsaptamyupmānāvyvādvitīyakṛtyāḥ* (*A* 6.2.2).
4. The commentatorial study reveals the force of application of the principle of *satiśiṣṭa* in determining accentuation of compounds.

5. The *satiśiṣṭa svara* is more forceful than the previously ordained *svara,* obviating the force of the *'para'* principle, if the *satiśiṣṭa* principle had not operated.
6. In examining the morphological and semantic factors in placing the accentuation of a compound, it is found that there is correspondence between the two.
7. Morphological factors such as kṛt preserve the natural accentuation of the compound.
8. On the other hand *'kta'* is seen to bring about *antodātta* but is susperceded by the influence of *vibhakti* and then brings about *prakṛtisvara.*
9. *Nañ* is consistent in obviating the *bv-svara* and causes *antodātta.*
10. *Vibhakti* is a decidedly semantic influence that preserves the *prakṛtisvara,* obviating the *antodātta* (A 6.1.223).

These observations arc corroborated by the supporting evidence of the traditional commentators. The unique observation of the study lies in the synthesis of a grammatical operation, the *samāsānta* affixation and the inevitable and consequent process of accentuation in a *samāsa.*

## II. Summary and Discussion :

A review of the literature has revealed patent evidences to substantiate the influence of morphology and semantics on phonology. In his thesis for kṛt accentuation M.D. Balasubrahmaniam (1981) argued for the phonemic contrast provided by suprasegmentals such as *svara,* in instances such as *"ārya".*

The unique observations of this thesis lie in relating the complexity of accentuation as deduced from the *A* and its commentaries. As this thesis is very much exploratory in nature and preliminary in content, the basis for evidence has been taken from the traditional commentaries. The compositional suffixes have been dealt with extensively with regard to Indo European accentuation (Ghosh, 1938). Indeed, Wackernagel (1905) spends much space in *Altindische Grammatik* on the nature of the *samāsānta-s*.

However, works on the precise nature of compositional suffixation and accentuation of compounds in Sanskrit are not readily available till date to us. Our initial survey leads us to an encouraging premise that the *A* itself could serve as the basis for exploring these relations. Thus the *A* and its commentatorial tradition are used as the internal evidence to provide for a synthetic thesis.

An analysis of the individual morphemes that influence accentuation reveals that the process is not simplistic. In fact, there exist contradictions to the maxim of the unitary accent on compounds (e.g. *Bṛhaspáti)*. The complexity lies in that particles such as *kṛt, kta, nañ* and case affixes *(vibhakti)* influence accentuation often in antagonistic effect.

*Kṛt* retains the *prakṛtisvara* (negating *samāsāntodātta)*. This property was recorded with meticulous detail by M.D. Balasubrahmaniam (1981). *Kta* as a participle when it is incorporated in a compound contributes to *antodātta*. However, with the influence of *vibhakti* of a compound, it brings about *prakṛtisvara*. This is reflected in the *vārttika* on *(A* 6.2.2) where Kātyāyana mentions *kta* as a conditioning factor in bringing about *antodātta*.

The case of nañ is unique and of much interest as it exerts both a semantic and morphological influence on accentuation.

*Nañ* consistently influences accentuation as *antodātta*. This too was recorded by Kātyāyana as an exception to *bv-svara*. Our studies in this area are only of a preliminary nature. This area of negation in accentuation holds much promise.

The area of negation has been a much explored one especially with specific reference to the illustration अब्राह्मणः.

In the *Mbh,* Patañjali maintains that negation is semantic

in contributing a negative sense. However, Mithilesh Caturvedi's expatiation in the study of *Vṛttisamuddeśa* provides insight into various expositions on the area according to the different schools of thought. Bhartrhari, is said to be of the opinion that the negative particle is indicative *(dyotaka)* and not expressive. Whether the nañ particle is semantic or not is a controversial topic among the various schools of thought (cf. Caturvedi, 2001).

In this study, a relationship of the morphological role of nañ in accentuation is obvious. A semantic function can be adduced but further studies remain to be done before a consensus can come about with regard to the semantic nature of nañ in *samāsasvara.* However, our studies do support the 'indicative' *(dyotaka)* function of nañ in its minimal function as a *sememe.*

The semantics of case-affixation in Sanskrit have most often been dealt with respect to syntax. This study is unique in that we have attempted to demonstrate the influence of *vibhakti* on accentuation. *Kātyāyana* was probably the first to take note of the antagonistic influences of *negation* and *vibhakti* on accentuation. Also, the effect of semantic conditioning on accentuation, is highlighted in such instances where the explicit meaning of a word influences accentuation. Moreover, such profoundly linguistic features as *vibhakti* based on their semantic relations also patently influence accentuation.

One is aware of the fact that Patañjali refers to the difficulty of ascertaining *"desired accentuation"* in *'tripadabahuvrīhi-s'* when *samāsānta* is taken into account. However, by pointing out that *samāsāntodātta* contributes to the accentuation of the 'internal *tp*\ Patañjali also does implicate a relationship between compositional suffixation and accentuation. It is this complexity that made us take up this area for scrutiny in the backdrop of evidence from the *A* and the commentaries. Our studies do show the greater degree of difficulty in accentuation in *bv-s* even in two membered *samāsa-s.* Although the relationship between *samāsānta* and accentuation is not simplistic as implied by *samāsasya (A* 6.1.223), the presence of an interrelationship between *samāsānta* suffixation and accentuation is an unequivocal one. All the *sūtra-s* pertaining to different morphological and semantic influences are read together to form a case for *samāsānta* suffixation and accentuation in *samāsa-s*. Thus, we find that our evidence justifies the extensive criticism of Patañjali in *Samarthāhnika,* inspite of the critique on the accentuation of many membered compounds. He also maintains that the two aspects of *samāsānta* and accentuation are inter-related by repeatedly referring to the influences of the *samāsānta* suffixation and the problems thereof. In Chapter 1 the problems of many membered compounds vis-a -vis accentuation was addressed to point out the increasing complexity of this inter-relationship. Still, one is aware from the evidence culled that in spite of the complexity of accentuation, there exists a direct relationship between *samāsānta* suffixation and accentuation in two memebered *samāsa-s*.

The demonstration of the above relationships in the accentuation of a compound, we hope, is our preliminary contribution in the area of accentuation.

The phonological and semantic correspondences of a language have been highlighted by many linguists including Chomsky, and was mentioned in the chapter titled "Review of Literature". Stockwell's revised theory is that there need not be a one to one correspondence between surface and deep structures. Indeed, one can find a semantic network of complexity in the deep structure that supports a dynamic accentuation (suprasegmentals) of a compound in word-formation. It is likely that correspondences can be decisively laid out for the accentuation of compounds (as deduced from the *A)* and its underlying semantic motivations, although a one to one correspondence is unlikely. While we are aware of Schmerling's (1976) opinion that stress is not necessarily contrastive in languages such as English, in treating the accent of the *Chandas* to be the pitch accent we have taken cognizance of works such as those of M.D. Balasubrahmaniam where in it has been demonstrated that in the *Chandas* the pitch is held to be contrastive.

In this thesis, a preliminary atiempt has been made to throw light on the relationship and interdependence of semantics and accentuation, devolved from the internal evidence in P's *A*. The evidence comes from the mode in which his *sūtra-s* are arranged, defined and inter-related. Supporting evidence is culled from the traditional commentaries, especially, those of the *Pāṇini-ya* tradition. S.D. Laddu's seminal article on the nature of the *bhāṣā* and vedic during P's time are not taken *in toto* but are powerful arguments for the fact that accent was a viable dynamic of language during the time of *P*.

From the above observations we conclude that both semantic and morphological factors influence the accentuation of compounds in compound word formation. The inter-relationship of *samāsānta* to *udātta* as detailed in the *Samarthāhnika* is elaborately detailed, justified and critiqued in the light of latter day commentators as well. Thus the devolution of *samāsāntodātta* is brought about by a complex series of steps of which the *samāsānta* and *udātta* are only parts but together contribute to the unitary accent of the whole compound.

# BIBLIOGRAPHY

## ARTICLES AND BOOKS


Allea, W.S. — Some Prosodic aspects of Retroflexion and Aspiration in Sanskrit, Bulletin of the School of Oriental and African Studies, Vol. 13, pp 939-46, 1951.

Retroflexion in Sanskrit - Prosodic techniques and its relevance to comparative statement, Bulletin of the school of Oriental and African studies, Vol. 16, Part III, pp. 556-65, 1954.

Anathanarayana, H.S. — Some problems in Vedic accentuation, Indian Antiquary, III, Series IV, 55-61, 1971.

Balasubrahnraniam, M.D. — An accentual note on vikata in Pāṇini and the Veda, Indian Linguistics, Vol. 26, p. 18, 1965.

A System of Kṛt Accentuation in Pāṇini and the Veda, Rashtriya Sanskrit Vidyapeetha, Tirupathi 1981.

Benfey, Th. — Complete Grammar of Sanskrit

Grammar, Leipzig, 1862; A Short Grammar for Beginners, Leipzig, 1855.

Bhattacharya, Vidusekhara. Chandas, Journal of Ganganatha Jha Research Institute, Vol.-1, ii, Allahabad, 1944.

Böhtlingk, Otto. Pāṇini's Grammatik, Motilal Banarsidass Publishers Ltd., 2000.

Ein ersten Versuchuver den accent in Sanskrit, Mem. Petersburg, VI. 7 :1 114,1848.

Bolinger, Dwight. Rime, Assonance and Morpheme Analysis, Word, 6, 117-36, 1950.

A theory of Pitch Accent in English, Word, 14, 109-49, 1958.

Contrastive Accent and Contrastive stress, Language, 37, 83-96, 1961a.

Ambiguities in Pitch Accent, Word 1961b.

Accent is predictable (If you're a mind -reader). Langauge. 48, 633-44, 1972.

Intonation across Languages, "Universals of Human Language 2 : Phonology" ed. by Joseph H. Greenberg, 471-524, Stanford University Press, Stanford, 1978.

Intonation and its parts, Language, 48:505-33, 1982.

Bopp, F. A Critical Grammar of Sanskrit Language, abridged second edition, Berlin, 1845.

Bresnan, Joan. Sentence Stress and Syntatic Transformations, Language, 47:2571-81, 1971.

Stress and Syntax : A Reply, Language 48 : 326-42, 1972.

Brugmann, K. A Comparative Grammar of Indo-Germanic Languages, Vol II, p.l, 1891.

Burrow, T. The Sanskrit Language, Faber and Faber, London, 1959

Cardona, G. The bhāṣikā accentuation system, Studien zur Indologie und Iranistik, Band 18,1993.

Pāṇini, A Survey of Research, Motilal Banarsidass Publishers, New Delhi, 1980.

Linguistic Analysis and Some Indian Traditions, Bhandarkar Oriental Research Insitute, Pune, 1983.

Pāṇini, His work and its traditions-Volume-I, Motilal Banarsidass Publishers, New Delhi,1997.

Recent Research in Pāṇinian Studies, Motilal Banarsidass Publishers, New Delhi,

Caturvedi, Mithilesh Vṛttisamuddeśa of Bhartṛhari's Vakyapadiya, Shivalik Prakashan, 2001.

Chomsky, Noam and F. Linkoff. On Accent and Juncture in English in M. Halle and Roman Jakobson, Mouton, 1956.

Chomsky, Noam and Halle, Morris. The Sound Pattern of English, Harper and Row, 1956.

Crystal, David. Prosodic Systems and Intonation in Eiiglish, Cambridge University Press, Cambridge 1969.

The English Tone of Voice: ed. by Edward Arnold. 1975.

Dash, Siniruddha. The Syntax and Semantics of Sanskrit Nominal Compounds, University of Madras Publication, 1992.

Devasthali, G.V. Anubandhas of Pāṇini, Pune, 1967.

Ghosh, Batakrishna. Linguistic Introduction to Sanskrit, Sankrit Pustak Bhandar, 1988.

Gray J.E.B. An Analysis of Rg Vedic Recitation, Bulletin of the School of Oriental and African Studies, Volume - 22, i, 86-94, 1959.

An Analysis of Namboodiri Ṛg Veda recitation and the nature of Vedic accent, Bulletin of the School of Oriental and African studies, Volume - 22, iii, 499-530,1959.

Guy, Gregory and von Willer, Julia. The Meaning of Intonation in Australian English, Australian Journal of Linguistics, 4: 1-17, 1984.

Hadding - Koch, Kerstin and Studdert, M. Kennedy An Experimental Study of Some Intonation Contours, Phonetica, 11,175-85, 1964.

Halliday, Michael. A.K. Intonation and Grammar in British English, The Hague, Mouton, 1967a.

Harnish, Robert, M. Meaning and Speech Acts ( A Review of Katz), Lingua, 49, 331-54 1977a.

Householder, Fred.W. Accent, Juncture, Intonation and My Grandfather's Reader, V/ord 13, 234-45, 1957.

Jesperson, Otto. Negation in English and other Languages (2nd Edition 1966) : Ejnar Munksgaard.

Joshi, S.D. *Amṛtadhārā, Prof. R.N. Dandekar Felicitation Volume* 1984.

Kempson, R.M. *Semantic Theory*, Cambridge, 1977.

Kiparsky, Paul. *Some Theoretical Problems in Pāṇini's Grammar*, Bhandarkar Oriental Research Insitute, Punc, 1982.

Kurylowicz, Jerzy. L'accentuation des langues indoeuropéenne (Krakow), 1958.

Ladd, Robert, D. The Structure of Intonational meaning, Indiana University Press, Bloomington, 1980.

Laddu, S.D. The *laukika*, *vaidika* and *yājñika* accentuation with the Munitraya of Sanskrit Grammar, Dandekar Felicitation volume, 93-111, 1969.

Lahiste, Ilse. *Suprasegmentals*, Cambridge, MA: MIT Press, 1970.

Liberman, Mark and Prince, Alan. On Stress and Linguistic Rythmn, Linguistic Inquiry, 8, 249-336, 1977.

Lieberman, Philip. Intonation Perception and Language, Cambridge MA, MIT Press, 1967.

Lyons, John. Semantics, Cambridge University Press, Cambridge, 1993

Mahavira. Treatment of Samāsa in Pāṇini, Seminar on Pāṇini, Kurukshelra University, 1972.

Macdonell, A.A. Vedic Grammar, Strassburg,1910.

Mayrhofer, M. A. Sanskrit Grammar, Translation of *Sanskrit Grammatik*, University of Alabama Press, 1972.

Meillet. Sur L'Accent Védique, Bulletin de La Societés Linguistique de Paris, Vol 34, (1934).

Mishra, Vidhata. *A Critical Study of Sanskrit Phonetics*, Chaukhamba Sanskrit Pratishthan, Viiranasi. I972.

Miiller, Max. *A Sanskrit Grammar for Beginners*, London 1866.

Murti, Srimannarayana. *Sanskrit Compounds, A Philosophical Study*, Chaukhamba Sanskrit Pratishthan, Varanasi, 1974.

Newman, Stanley, S. On the Stress System of English, Word 2, 171 - 87, 1946.

O'Connor, J.D. and Arnold, J.F. *Intonation of Colloquial English*, Longmans Green & Co., London, 1961.

Pandit, M.D. *A Concordance of Vedic Compounds Interpreted by Veda* (Vol. I), Centre of Advanced Study in Sanskrit, University of Pune, Silver Jubilee Year, Pune, 1989.

Pike, Kenneth L. *The Intonation of American English*, Ann Arbor, University of Michigan Press, 1945.

Raja, Kunhan C. The relation of accent and meaning, Proceedings of the 5th All India Oriental Conference, Lahore, 1928.

Renou, L. Etude deegrammaire Sanskrite Première Série, Adricn Maissonneuve, Paris, 1936.

Bibliographie Védique Paris, 1931.

Roland, Harweg. Kompositum und Katalysationstext Vornchmlich im Späteren Sanskrit, Mouton Janue Linguarum, 1964.

Sankaran, C.R. Accentual Variations in Relation to Semantic Variation, Kuppuswamy Commemoration Volume, 1935.

Schmerling, Susan F. Aspects of English sentence Stress, Austin, University of Texas Press, 1976.

Scmitt, Alfred. *Musikalischer Akzent und antike*, Metrik, 1953.

Sehgal S.R. Importance of Accent in the Vedas, Poona Orientalist, 6 (1941).

Selkirk, Elizabeth, 0. The role of prosodic categories in English word stress, Linguistic Inquiry, 11, 563-605, 1980a.

On prosodic structure and its relation to syntatic structure, Indiana University Linguistics Club, Bloomington, 1980b.

Al George,Sergin. On Negative Compounds, A Parallel between Pāṇini and Aristotle,

CASS Studies, pp 137-140, Pune, 1983.

Sharma, Dipti. Structure and Meaning, Nag Publishers, 1982.

Speijer, T. Sanskrit Syntax, Leiden, 1896.

Staal, J.F. Room at the top in Sanskrit, Indo-Iranian Journal, The Hague, Volume 9, pp. 165-198.,1966.

Ritual and Mantras, Rules without Meaning, Motital Banarsidass Publishers Private Limited, Delhi, 1983.

Nambudiri Veda recitation, Amsterdam, 1961.

Stockwell, Robert. The Role of Intonation; Reconsiderations and other considerations, "Intonation" ed. by Dwight Bolinger, 87-109, Harmondsworth: Penguin, 1972.

Subrahmanyam, P.S. Deep Structure and Surface Structure in Pāṇini, All India Conference of Linguistics, 3:20-21, 1972.

Pāṇinian Linguistics, Institute for the Study of Languages and Cultures of Asia and Africa, Tokyo University of Foreign Studies, 1999.

Thieme, Paul. Pāṇini and Veda, Allahabad, Globe Press, 1935.

Varma, Siddeswar. The broad features of the Vedic accent, Journal of the U.P. Historical Society, Vol. 18, Parts 1 and 2, 6-15, 1945.

The Vedic accent and the interpreters of Pāṇini, Journal of the Bombay branch of Royal Asiatic Society, Vol. 26, i, pp. 1-9, 1951.

The Vedic concept of Metres, All India Oriental Conference, 16th Session, Lucknow Proceedings, pp 10-19.

Wackernagel, J. Altindische Grammatik, II Enleitung zur Worllehrc Nominalkomposition, Göttingen, Vandenhoeck and Ruprecht, 1905. Reprinted, 1957.

Whitney, W.D. Journal of American Oriental Society, 5, 1865.

**Traditional Works (as per chronological order)**

Swami Prahlad Cari ed. Vedantakesari *Aṣṭādhyāyī-Sūtrapāṭha*, Krishnadas Academy, Vuranasi, 1985.

Vasu, S.C. *Aṣṭādhyāyī of Pāṇini*, Volumes I and II, Motilal Banarsidass Publishers. Delhi, 1997.

Katre, S.M. *Aṣṭādhyāyī of Pāṇini*, Motilal Banarsidass Publishers, Delhi, 1989.

Yudhisthira Mimamsaka *Uṇādikoṣaḥ*, Ramlal Kapoor Trust Press, 1987.

Sukla, Sri Kalikaprasada Ed.Paribhāṣenduśekhara, Sampurnananda Samskrit Viswavidyalaya, Varanasi, 1991.

K.V. Abhyankar and J.M. Shukla Vyākaraṇamahābhasya of Patañjāli, Paspaśāhnika (Ahnikas 1 & 2), The Cultural Centre Research & Publication, Department of Sanskrit Vidya, Parisamstha Poona, 1968.

Sri Bhargava Sastri Joshi. Vyākaranamahābhāṣya of Patañjali, volumes 4 and 5 with the Pradīpoddyota, Chaukhamba Sanskrit Pratishthan, 1991.

Joshi, S.D. and Roodbergen. J.A.F. J.A.F. Patañjali's Vyākaraṇa Mahābhāṣya, Samarthāhnika, University of Poona, Pune, 1968.

Joshi, S.D. and Roodbergen J.A.F. Patañjali's Vyākaraṇa Mahābhāṣya. Avyayībhāvatatpuruṣāhnika, University of Poona, Pune, 1969.

Patañiali's Vyākaraṇa Mahābhāṣya, Bahuvrīhidvandvāhnika, University of Poona, Pune, 1974.

Jaya Sankar Lal Tripathi. Kāśikā, A commentary of Pāṇini's Grammar, Vol. 6-7, Tara Book Agency, Varanasi, 1990.

Sarma, Raghunatha P. Vākyapadīyam, Part III Vṛttisamuddeśa, Chaukhamba Sanskrit Pratishthan, Varanasi 1977.

Vasu, S.C. Siddhānta Kaumudī of Bhattoji Dīksita, Vol. II, Motilal Banarsidass Publishers, New Delhi, 1982.

Giridharasarma Caturvedi and Paramesvara Yidhyabhaskara Vaiyākaranasiddhāntakaumudi (bālamanoramā tattvabodhinīsahitā) Motilal Banarasidass Publishers, New Delhi, 1991.

Devasthali, G.V. Svarasiddhāntamañjarī, Bhandarkar Oriental Research Insitute, Pune, 1983.

Abhyankar, K.V. Svarā Prakriyā, Ānandāśrama, Pune, 1896.

Abhyankar, T.B. Svaramañjarī, Pune, 1946.

Sastri, Sivaramakrishna, K.A. Svarasiddhānta Candrikā, Madras. Law Journal Press, Mylapore, Madras, 1936.

# INDEX OF IMPORTANT TECHNICAL TERMS AND WORKS

# INDEX OF ANCIENT AND MODERN AUTHORS

★★★